NEST EGG

HOW TO BUILD YOURS... THEN TURN IT INTO SOMETHING EXTRAORDINARY

NEST EGG
How to Build Yours ...
Then Turn It into Something Extraordinary

BY JEFF GOBLE

Edited by Carol Powers
Designed by Brian Grubb
Copy edited by Robert Campbell

ROCKHILL
B O O K S

Published by Rockhill Books, an imprint
of Kansas City Star Books
1729 Grand Blvd.
Kansas City, Missouri 64108
All rights reserved.
Copyright © 2015 by Jeffrey Goble

First Edition, First Printing
ISBN: 978-1-61169-160-3
Library of Congress Control Number:
2015937045
Printed in the United States of America
by Walsworth Publishing Co., Inc.,
Marceline, Missouri

Available for purchase at Amazon.com.

TABLE OF CONTENTS

DEDICATION

For my Mom and Dad, my bride, Sharon, and sons
Corban, Clark and Andrew. Thank you for your constant love,
encouragement and support of my passions.

This is for you.

FOREWORD

You might enjoy a cup of coffee or a glass of iced tea as you sit down to read "Nest Egg" because it is like having a conversation about your life with a friend.

Jeff shares – in simple terms and ordinary language – stories and lessons from his more than 30 years of experience in investment strategy. We see how he arrived at the practices that have served him and his employer so well and that have helped many of his personal clients attain great wealth. But more than that, he offers a commentary on what money is for.

Jeff and his family are longtime members of Village Presbyterian Church in Prairie Village, where I am senior pastor. This has afforded the opportunity for a number of stimulating discussions about the relationship between one's money and one's life, although I take no credit for Jeff's inclination to generosity.

But, as Jeff understands, it is not what we squirrel away but what we give away, that creates real financial security. If you wish to grow your investments, you will find help in these pages.

More than that, you will find an invitation to plan not only what you can make in the markets, but the difference you can make in the world. There is practical wisdom here but the spirit of the book is joy.

A truth of life is that it is impossible to be generous and grumpy at the same time.

Rev. Tom Are, Jr.
Senior Pastor
Village Presbyterian Church
Prairie Village, Kansas

The house always wins when it comes to interest rates, but when it comes to liquidity and the fixed income markets, decisions require a steady hand.

I have worked alongside Jeff Goble my entire professional career and as the CEO of UMB, I am ultimately responsible for investing our bond portfolio, which at our company represents half of our balance sheet. This is a very important task and requires a great deal of regular, thoughtful diligence.

We have an exceptional team. Jeff is a very important member of that team. His is a voice of reason, reflecting decades of experience. His close observation of the annals of banking and long view of the markets shape his thoughts about how to protect hard-earned cash today.

When it comes to economic data, it is easy to come by popular sentiment. And it is just as easy to find a contrarian. What is hard to find is sound, independent advice. Why? Well, because often it requires boldness and great conviction.

As you will see in Chapter 11, Jeff had a very close business and personal relationship with my father. Chapter 10 is about my dear friend Christine Lynn and her wonderfully generous nature.

If you seek independent, sound counsel, listen to Jeff.

Mariner Kemper
Chairman and Chief Executive Officer
UMB Financial Corporation

INTRODUCTION

It has been said that once you start something, you're more than half-way done. Congratulations on taking the first step!

Many people place creating a financial plan and using it to build a nest egg for themselves and their families high on their "to do" lists, but too often they procrastinate and sometimes never get around to it.

Wherever you are financially today, I strongly urge you to start this project now and allocate ample time for it – since time itself is one of the most powerful multipliers in your financial success. Treat your plan like the very important part-time job that it is, requiring discipline, regular attention and frequent fine-tuning. Most of your success will depend on you.

And, trust me, you'll find that most satisfying. As Henry Ford once said, "If you chop your own wood, it will warm you twice."

If, however, you delve into this book and recognize that you simply do not have the interest or commitment for the process, I recommend that you hire a professional money manager to help you navigate the markets and build your nest egg.

Thousands of qualified financial planners are available and whatever you pay in fees may be more than worth it. Ask your most successful friends for referrals.

One other option you may wish to consider is to begin on your own, and then partner with an expert, either full- or part-time, as your nest egg grows in size and complexity.

If you decide to first go it alone (and I am hoping you will at least try!) you must be willing to educate yourself about how successful investment plans work, learn the language of financial transactions, and seek guidance and wisdom from experienced investors.

I am so fortunate that my work has given me a bird's eye view of the experience of thousands of investors over the past 35 years. My clients have had nest eggs ranging from thousands of dollars to hundreds of millions.

Why should you care, you ask, how someone got hundreds of millions? *Because the investing principles and strategies for thousands and hundreds of millions may have many similarities.* The results vary only by the number of zeroes.

I've also had the opportunity to watch many different investment styles and philosophies at work. The best learning opportunities, by far, have been when markets became volatile or fell dramatically and unexpectedly.

It's then, as you will see in Chapter 9, when those primal emotions – fear and greed – can create panic decisions that expose weak investment strategies. In the following chapters, I will pass along some keys to success in turbulent financial times.

The most fulfilling part of my career, by far, has been the personal and professional relationships developed over three decades at UMB Bank. They become more important to me each day. The most gratifying parts of life always involve the people you care about most. It took me a while to figure this out, so I encourage you to accelerate your learning curve on this if you can.

I am lucky to have had the privilege to pursue things I enjoy and am passionate about for my entire career, and to meet and learn from so many intelligent and generous people. The "Pearls of Wisdom" scattered throughout the book are a few wise investment sayings I've collected along the way.

Many of my most wealthy clients have commented that once their nest egg is built, it is twice as much fun to donate some of it to meaningful, sometimes even life-changing causes.

There are many births, weddings, anniversaries and, sadly, funerals in one's professional and personal life. It is the circle of life, so try not to rush things, and enjoy each day as much as you possibly can.

Four things will most likely determine your success in building a nest egg: 1) when you start, 2) how much you invest each month, 3) the mix of investments you select, and 4) how you react when markets turn volatile.

Over the next 12 chapters, I will lay out a systematic plan that may help you attempt to become a successful, long-term investor, build your nest egg, and then explore some ways to turn your success into something extraordinary.

That last will be the fun part. Trust me.

Jeffrey Goble

NEST EGG

CHAPTER ONE

LET'S GET ORGANIZED!

Choose a record-keeping system that can grow with you.

The Commitment

The critical first step in building a nest egg for your family is making a simple personal commitment: to stay current and follow through with your financial plan. My experience tells me this is the single most important predictor of your financial success.

Unfortunately, many people start this process with the best of intentions and then over time lose enthusiasm or interest. I see my principal job as encouraging you to stick to your long-term nest egg building plan.

The second step is to select a method for organizing your financial statement, investments and records. The goal is to create structure and focus for building your nest egg, as if it was an evening or weekend part-time job. You want to make it a fun and educational part of your life routine.

Making a simple balance sheet for your family is a great starting point. You'll have to decide whether you want to maintain your records on paper or electronically. Every person is different in this regard and either method will work. Keep in mind that you will be updating this record frequently over the years ahead. Electronic or digital record keeping can make updates easier.

Nest Egg Software

Many people start their nest egg record-keeping on paper and then transition to an electronic system. Many excellent software programs are available when, and if, you go electronic.

The Wall Street Journal published a list of software options Nov. 28, 2014. Check them out to identify the best fit for you:

1 Brokerage or mutual fund families
2 Vanguard Group's "Portfolio Watch"
3 Fidelity Investments' "Guided Portfolio Summary"

4 Charles Schwab's "Portfolio Checkup"
5 Morningstar "Premium"
6 Personal Capital Software
7 Sigfig Wealth Management

For the long term, I think an electronic tracking system is the way to go. Once you are comfortable with the security and performance capabilities of the investment software you select, it simply saves you time and effort.

Your nest egg hopefully will expand in size and complexity over the years, so think ahead about selecting a system that can grow with you. You will want to find one that allows you to compare and appreciate the growth that hopefully will occur from month to month and year to year. That is the fun and gratifying part of your personal involvement.

My family started with a simple three-ring notebook binder and a quarterly balance sheet in 1981. Don't be discouraged if you have only a few assets to list at the outset. That is normal for anyone starting out after completing an education and beginning to pay back student loans or other debts.

After graduate school, I can remember listing furniture, my wife's engagement ring and even lawn mowers as assets to offset the student loans on the liability side. We were driven to make the net worth balance turn positive and then grow as quickly as possible as we paid off education loans. I saw this as our first great financial challenge as newlyweds.

As we gained experience, we switched from a notebook system to an electronic system that could make pie charts and perform other analysis. The system is your choice but make sure it can answer, in the quickest and easiest way, the 50,000-foot question – "How is our nest egg doing today?"

Many investors select the start of each month to collect brokerage and bank statements and update their nest egg position. It's a logical time, as you will just have received last month's statements in the mail or can sign onto your accounts on the Internet to get your numbers.

An added benefit of keeping your balance sheet current is that it makes it easy to complete applications for home equity loans, car loans, mortgages or credit cards. Your financial information will always be correct and easy to access.

Trust me, you will make a good impression on lenders and credit card companies if you are super organized and up to date with your financial records when you meet or apply to borrow money. Act like it is no big deal to be well prepared and you will sail through these encounters.

The Balance Sheet

The rather obvious goal of making a balance sheet for your family is to establish a starting point for building your nest egg.

You know that A (assets) minus B (debts or liabilities) balances to equal C (nest egg or net worth). There are several ways to create the same positive result, a steadily growing C.

Your first task is to make a plan to start investing and growing your assets as quickly and as safely as possible. Second is to focus on paying off any debt you have.

The smartest thing to do in reducing your debt is to stop leaving balances on credit cards every month. Credit cards are the most expensive and addictive form of debt. A very important early goal is to try to keep your monthly fixed expenses, your "nut," as small as possible.

This discipline will make it easier to invest regular amounts each month, as if you were making payments on things you have purchased. This is the "pay yourself first" concept. It will serve you well when you decide to retire from the working world.

It's normal to be curious about where you should be, nest egg-wise, at various stages of life. There's no really good answer to that question because there are too many personal variables. But there are some widely accepted nest egg benchmarks based on an investor's age, so maybe that is a good starting point.

Forbes Magazine, for example, uses Federal Reserve Bank research data to publish savings benchmarks based on yearly income. See page 6 for the latest benchmarks.

Continued on page 6

THE BALANCE SHEET
(at Market Value)

A S S E T S

Cash

Stocks

Bonds/ CDs

Real Estate

Autos

401K

IRA Accounts

Furniture/Art

Cash Value of
Life Insurance

Other Assets

L I A B I L I T I E S

Home Mortgage

Auto Loans

Student Loans

Credit Card Debt

Other Loans

N E T   W O R T H

Continued from page 4

SAVINGS BENCHMARKS

	Median Household INCOME	Median Family NET WORTH
Age 45-54	$63,861	$117,900
Age 55-64	$55,937	$179,400
Age 65-74	$33,118	$206,700

If you have more or less income than the averages, you can multiply the net worth totals by the same factor. This data will at least give you a starting point for comparison.

Full Disclosure

We live in a world that rightly values transparency, so I would like to take this opportunity to disclose one of the main reasons for any financial success we have achieved: my wife, Sharon.

We met while in graduate business school at the University of Kansas, where she earned a B.S. degree in Accounting, a Masters degree in Tax, and then became a CPA. It is safe to say she has strong financial credentials

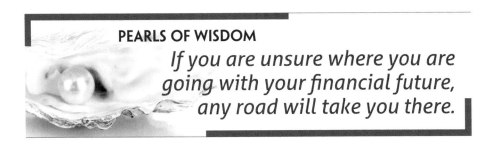

PEARLS OF WISDOM

If you are unsure where you are going with your financial future, any road will take you there.

and that numbers come easy for her. I have an MBA in Finance.

Our financial backgrounds undoubtedly gave us an advantage in building our nest egg. In the spirit of paying it forward, I want to share some of the strategies that have worked well for our family.

Sharon has her own list of basic life success/money management principles that we have adopted. I'll reveal those later in the chapter.

In marriage, I subscribe to the notion that two horses have to pull equally or the wagon will veer off the road. We have been happily married for 33 years...so no roadside ditches yet.

I also believe strongly in the happy spouse, happy life theory. We are a family-centered team and our goal is to make it financially possible for our children to follow their dreams, build strong families and pursue careers they love. We will ultimately expect them to turn parts of their nest eggs into things that make a difference.

We have three sons and set up a nest egg brokerage account for each shortly after he was born, using the Uniform Gifts to Minors provision. We opened accounts with Scout Brokerage in Kansas City, a division of UMB – obviously convenient for us. But many good brokerage firms are available.

We also used our state's college funding program (Kansas Learning Quest) to help save for college. Investing in the program also cut our state tax bill. For many years, we made automatic monthly investments to a wide variety of mutual funds for each son's brokerage and Learning Quest accounts.

Any gift to brokerage accounts set up for a child with you as custodian will pass legally and automatically to him or her at age 21. There are pros and cons to setting up brokerage accounts like we did. For starters, I encourage you to check with a tax expert.

As parents, we didn't own the accounts but we managed them and didn't tell the boys about them until each turned 21. It was certainly a fun surprise when we delivered the good news.

You should do research and evaluate the costs of maintaining brokerage accounts. For us, online access was critical, as was the ability to aggregate all of our brokerage accounts into one master summary page. That allowed us to see everything any time we wanted, with only one web page sign-on.

Plus, you can simply download your electronic monthly brokerage statements into your master software program. Simple is always better!

The Master Account Pie Chart

The next step in nest egg building is to make a list of all of your current investments from all of your brokerage statements and then break them out in a master account pie chart by type. Don't forget that one of your assets listed in the pie chart should be the equity (market value minus your mortgage and/or home equity loan) that you own in your home and autos. For this initial pie chart, keep the asset categories very broad as in the chart below.

I'm familiar with the standard banking industry norms for the maximum amount of debt one should carry. For example, your mortgage payment should never be higher than 28 percent of your monthly gross pay. Another widely accepted benchmark is that your total payments for all debt, including student loans and credit cards, should not exceed 36 percent of your monthly gross pay and/or income.

You can determine where you stand very easily by applying these benchmarks to your financial position and monthly bill paying process.

You should allow 34 percent of your gross monthly pay for taxes.

The final 30 percent is for fixed living expenses (food, medical and child care, gas, insurance, and any expenses that may arise unexpectedly), plus contributions to your nest egg account.

I have always felt that a reserve-for-bad-luck fund of at least six to nine months of your monthly expenses should be in a very safe place (like an FDIC-insured bank). It improves one's sleep.

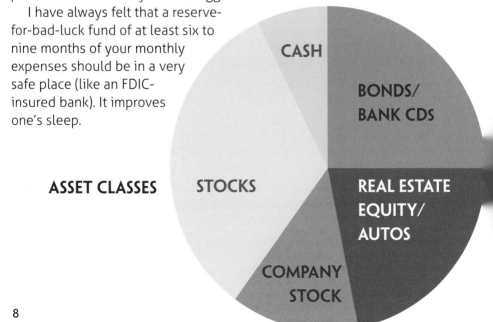

CASH

BONDS/
BANK CDS

ASSET CLASSES

STOCKS

REAL ESTATE
EQUITY/
AUTOS

COMPANY
STOCK

Finally, what you've been waiting for...

SHARON'S 10 RULES FOR FINANCIAL (AND LIFE) SUCCESS

1 Avoid depreciating assets like new cars (although they are very fun) as much as you can. If you buy new, buy a high-quality brand and take really good care of it. Otherwise, used cars at least two years old are a much better value.

2 Never do business with family members without signed contracts.

3 Use automated savings plans to build discipline for investing, and always live below your means.

4 Always have a minimum of six months' living expenses in safe and liquid investments.

5 Make sure your life insurance is of high quality and is the proper dollar amount. Life is unpredictable!

6 Education is the key to one's future.

7 Pay in cash whenever you can; you will probably spend less.

8 Review your will and estate plan at least once a year, as the rules are always changing. It pays to seek professional help in this area, as well as in preparing your tax returns each year.

9 Enjoy what you are doing or find something else. Life is short.

10 You can never have too many friends.

PEARLS OF WISDOM

The best markets are always the ones you can't seem to get in. The worst markets to enter, unfortunately, are usually the easiest to get in.

NEST EGG

CHAPTER TWO

LESSONS FROM THE BEST INVESTORS IN THE WORLD

Sometimes good investments can be made in things you understand and enjoy.

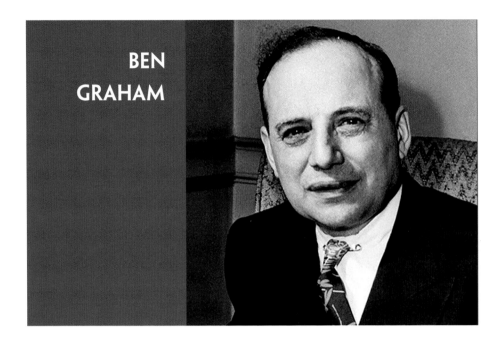

BEN GRAHAM

Are You 'Intelligent'?

There are many, many great investors in the world. The person I have learned the most from, however, is probably Benjamin Graham.

Graham is widely regarded as the father of value investing. His basic principles about diversification and the emotion of investing have greatly influenced my thinking and that of many others worldwide. First, a little background on Mr. Graham.

His famous book, "The Intelligent Investor," published in 1923, is a must read for anyone interested in understanding the basics of investing. I was particularly interested in his broad characterization of investors as either "passive" or "enterprising," and his definition of what it takes to be an intelligent investor.

Graham wrote that to be considered "intelligent," an investor must be patient, disciplined and eager to learn. Other required traits include the ability to harness your emotions and think for yourself. This all made perfect sense to me.

Passive vs. Enterprising Investing

Passive investors are more defensive by nature and generally are happy with the steady growth of their nest eggs, even if it means at a slower rate than more aggressive investing might bring. They simply do not want to bother with more complex investment strategies and prefer to spend little time managing their nest eggs. If this sounds like you, you might want to partner with a good wealth management advisor to develop a strategy for you. All you would do is review the quarterly results.

Enterprising investors, by contrast, are tolerant of the ups and downs of markets if it means a greater likelihood of higher returns over the long term. They are more willing to be actively engaged in their nest egg-building process. I think everyone needs to decide which investor profile best suits her or him. There is no right or wrong choice here. There may even be a middle ground, where you hire someone to do a portion of your nest egg management and control another part on your own.

I also like the concept of "margin of safety" that Graham championed throughout his life. In other words, the price you pay for any investment is critical in determining its long-term performance. One must be careful not to overpay, even for investments with very low risk. This applies to investments as well as real estate and other types of assets.

The basic premise of his value investing approach was that every investment has a price that can be too high or too low relative to its real worth, and one should seek out the price that creates a margin of safety if market conditions reverse, which they often will. If you buy something cheap enough, you generally worry less, as you have built in some price wiggle room.

One of Graham's most famous students, who we will discuss next, always says that he likes to "buy a dollar for 60 cents" to have a comfortable margin of safety.

Graham believed that at least 25 percent of one's nest egg should always be in very safe, liquid investments like cash and high quality bonds. The other 75 percent should be a mix of safe investments and riskier ones like stocks and real estate, depending where one is in his or her life. At no time should any investor have all his or her resources committed to higher risk investments. I concur.

Graham further believed that one should overweight (increase) investment in stocks when they are out of favor, for example, and underweight (decrease) investment when the market and positive sentiment are high. This is counter cyclical investing at its best.

Graham was a classic counter cyclical investor and he helped me start looking at things from the opposite view of the "herd." The market itself is a pendulum of emotion, from optimism to pessimism, and it is very important to step back from time to time and gauge current trends in an emotionless manner.

Today's availability of real time news and stock prices on TV, your tablet or your smart phone only elevates the pendulum swings, in my opinion. This can create great opportunities if you are prepared.

When the market starts to swing, make the most of it.

For me, those big-picture, "light bulb" moments usually occur when I am on a plane, on vacation or performing repetitive tasks like walking or mowing our lawn. They also seem to happen more when I am well rested.

There is a fascinating physiological explanation for why and how these "aha" moments occur. We will discuss these exceptional moments of clarity in greater depth in Chapter 9.

Another concept that struck a chord with me was Graham's premise that investors can't manage returns on individual stocks, but they can manage their overall risk. By determining and managing the optimum mix of stocks and bonds, one aims to build steady, long-term returns. This requires that your portfolio be adjusted occasionally to reposition the risk levels depending on the direction and movement of the markets and your stage in life. This is the rebalancing concept that we will discuss later in Chapter 7.

It may come as a shock from a man who realized enormous wealth from foresight and precision, but Graham also felt that each day, one should "do something creative, something foolish and something generous." This is perhaps my favorite guidance from Graham. To me, it means that investing is a means to accomplish great things for your family but also for other people, and it comes from a wise and thoughtful man who was among the best investors and teachers of all time.

WARREN BUFFETT

Most people have heard of Warren Buffett, also known as the "Oracle of Omaha." He is a living legend in the field of investing and is a Graham disciple. He calls Ben Graham's "The Intelligent Investor" the best book ever written on the subject. That is very high praise coming from Warren Buffett.

As you'd expect, there are a great many books written about Warren Buffett. One of my favorites is "Warren Buffett, the $59 Billion Philanthropist," produced by the staff at Forbes Magazine. It is a collection of articles written by and about Buffett.

It describes how Buffett started his investment journey when he was 11 by purchasing six shares of Cities Service Company (now CITCO) with his sister for $38 per share. The stock suddenly fell to $27 and then rose to $40 and Buffett cashed out. Several years later, the stock was priced over $200 and – before he was a teenager – Buffett had learned his first real world lesson in investing: Be patient and hold.

Buffett says his favorite holding period is "forever." I saw a recent interview in which he discussed the advantages of purchasing very high quality businesses and holding them as they grow and prosper. He focuses little time on daily or weekly changes in the Dow Jones Index and thinks about his investments over a very long-term horizon.

He diversifies risk at his holding company, Berkshire Hathaway, by owning many companies in multiple industries. He also is an enthusiastic advocate for the managers of his companies and their products. He selects great companies in strong industries and lets his managers do their thing. It is easy to see why his company has been so successful for so long.

It was instructive to learn the history of Berkshire Hathaway. The Hathaway Manufacturing Company was founded in 1888 in New Bedford, Massachusetts, by Horatio Hathaway, a China trader, with profits from whaling in the Pacific. The business of the company was milling cotton and it had boom and bust years. A 1955 merger joined the textile company with Berkshire Fine Spinning Associates, a milling company that had operated since the early 1800s. Buffett started buying shares in 1962 when he noticed a trading pattern in the stock when mills were closed.

Today, Berkshire Hathaway is one of the world's largest and most diverse companies, owning names like GEICO, Coca Cola, General Electric, Wells Fargo, Helzberg Jewelers and the newly formed Kraft Heinz Company.

Buffett's folksy annual letter to shareholders is a must read for any investor and all of them are posted on Berkshire's website at berkshire-hathaway.com. One of my all-time favorite quotes was in one of his newsletters: *"Only when the tide goes out do you ever know who is swimming naked."*

Berkshire's stock ticker is BRKA/BRKB because there are two classes of stock, A and B shares. At the time of this writing, the A shares had the most expensive price per share of any stock: $222,411 per share. The B shares are much more affordable but have no voting rights. We hold some B

Warren Buffet is a return customer at Dairy Queen, which is wholly owned by Berkshire Hathaway.

shares just to be part of the fun ride and also to get the annual letter to shareholders directly.

One of Warren Buffett's many companies is Dairy Queen. You can bet that he did his usual due diligence on the company before buying in. However, by all accounts, he was already a happy consumer, a fondness that the press has been gleefully documenting for decades. Thus, by buying the stock, Buffett was literally putting his money where his mouth is. Put another way, he was staying within what he calls his "circle of competence" – buying within an industry that he understands.

Because the press loves Buffett stories, his loyalties are well known. His favorite lunch spot reportedly is a family-style Italian restaurant called

PEARLS OF WISDOM

Markets always eventually move in such a way as to punish the largest numbers of greedy investors.

Piccolo Pete's that has been an Omaha fixture since 1934, and he enjoys playing many hours of weekly bridge. Card games are reputed to keep your mind sharp as you get older, and it seems to be working for Buffett, who is 85.

I really like this common-man approach to life and business, and the fact that Buffett is a multi-billionaire makes it more notable. There is never an indication that he is anything but humble and appreciative of his good fortune. His investments seem to mirror the "keep it simple" and well grounded Midwestern philosophy.

A few years ago, in the middle of the 2008-2009 mortgage meltdown that nearly forced our economy into something akin to the Great Depression of the 1930s, Warren was approached to help rescue Wall Street firms in trouble. He invested $5 billion in the plan to save Goldman Sachs, at very favorable terms. It sent a message to the markets that things would work out, as everyone knows the intense due diligence Buffett performs before purchasing a company.

I also find it telling that Buffett considers Chapter 8 in Ben Graham's "Intelligent Investor" as the "bedrock of my investing activities." Chapter 8 is "The Investor and Market Fluctuations," and we will review many of its themes in Chapter 8 of this book, so stay tuned. Buffett once said: "You make the best buys when people are overly fearful."

Warren Buffett is usually regarded as one of the world's all-time best investors. His record of steady returns at Berkshire Hathaway is nothing short of spectacular. I also admire his plan to donate most of his fortune to charity via the Bill and Linda Gates Foundation. Just think of the great things he can accomplish by parlaying his success into something much, much greater!

Wealth, after all, is a rich person's great opportunity.

PEARLS OF WISDOM

The longer it takes to understand an investment and how you will be paid back, the worse the investment is for your portfolio.

HOWARD
MARKS

When someone calls their book "The Most Important Thing: Uncommon Sense for the Thoughtful Investor," it grabs my attention. We are all looking for ways to turn the worthwhile investment guidance available today into a simple formula that can benefit our own nest egg-building process. Make it simple and easy to follow and I want to learn more!

Howard Marks is one of the managers of Oaktree Capital Management in Los Angeles. His approach complements Ben Graham's and Warren Buffett's very well. While each person has his or her own unique road to investing success, the paths are all headed in the same direction and often intersect and overlap. As of August 18, 2015, Oaktree Capital managed 39 of the 50 state retirement funds in the U.S., according to its website.

Oaktree's general investment mantra under Mr. Marks is to find ways to achieve superior performance while incurring less-than-commensurate risk. In other words, they want to at least match the upside to the stock market in good years but also beat the market in down market years – an obvious winning strategy, especially for pension fund investors.

Their formula for success includes finding inefficiencies in pricing due to the herd paying too much or too little for certain types of out-of-favor or undervalued investments. In other words, they are bargain hunters.

Marks says that being part of the herd psychology is a formula for disaster. Like Benjamin Graham, Marks sees that markets swing from excessive optimism to excessive pessimism, often creating periods in which assets can be priced below their intrinsic, or fair, value.

Avoid the herd mentality.

What's in a Formula

In the later chapters of his book, Marks does an excellent job of explaining several more complex terms often seen today in investment industry literature. These are good terms for you to know in order to stay current with your reading homework assignments.

For example, here is Howard Marks' formula for estimating your portfolio's performance:

$$Y = A + Bx$$

Translated:

$$Y = A + Bx$$

performance, = skill + risk relative to the market times the or return   stock market's return as a whole.

Key to terms: Y = Return of the portfolio
A = Alpha, or return greater than the benchmark
B = Beta, or risk relative to the market
X = Market's average return

So, if the stock market returns 10 percent on average and your portfolio's risk relative to the market (Beta) is 1.5, your portfolio should return 15 percent. You will often read about "low Beta" or "high Beta" stocks or mutual funds. This formula allows you to actually quantify mathematically the reduced or additional leverage these funds may be using in comparison to their respective benchmarks. Some of the nest egg software options I discussed in Chapter 1 will do all of this, and more, for you automatically.

Alpha is the skill you hopefully add by selecting an experienced portfolio manager instead of just having your funds in an unmanaged market index or passive investment.

You will often see articles or investment columns entitled "Seeking Alpha," referring to the skill a particular manager might possess versus unmanaged, or index funds. In general, the more consistent Alpha produced by a manager over a long time horizon, the better! It is not an easy task to consistently beat the market. In fact, not even Warren Buffett does it every year.

Marks also developed what he calls his "Two-by-Two Matrix," which further summarizes the goals of aggressive and defensive investors.

Aggressive Investors	Defensive Investors
Without skilled investment advice	
Gain a lot when the market goes up but lose a lot when it goes down.	Don't lose much when the market goes down but don't gain much when market goes up.
With skilled investment advice	
Gain a lot when the market goes up but don't lose to the same degree when the market goes down.	Don't lose much when the market goes down but capture a fair bit of the gain when the market goes up.

Conclusions

The theories and practices of these three investors form the bedrock, as Buffett calls it, of my stock investing education. I hope you benefit from knowing a little more about how they came to their opinions. Together, they provide an excellent formula for long-term success. You can apply many of the same classic theories to bonds, as I will do later.

NEST EGG

CHAPTER

THREE

THE ART OF
DIVERSIFICATION

A horseshoe on the author's office wall always points up for good luck.

What's In Your Mix?

You may remember one of Benjamin Graham's investing basics from the previous chapter: One can only manage risk, not returns. One way to manage risk is through diversification, known in the investment industry as "asset allocation."

High quality bonds, cash and certificates of deposit issued by FDIC-insured banks are the assets primarily used for safety and income. They are your safety net and provide dry gunpowder when equity markets are volatile, which is, by the way, most of the time. I think of them as a rainy day fund in case good investment opportunities come along.

I do not agree with the theory that all of your cash should be working hard – or fully invested – all of the time. You will miss many opportunities that present themselves when others panic.

Individual stocks or stock mutual funds are designed for the long-term growth of your nest egg and for beating the rate of inflation. An important key to consistent, long term investing success *is appropriately managing the percentage allocation for each asset class in your portfolio over your life.* This was number three of my four keys to success listed in the introduction to this book, and as Ben Graham stated, one can only manage risk.

Asset allocation is a broad and complex subject that's been researched extensively. Wall Street firms and academia both seek to uncover the optimum mix for your nest egg. Basically, the goal of asset allocation is to find the perfect, yet dynamic, mix of investments, given one's age, risk tolerance and the "relative value" of the markets at any point in time.

We are *all* searching for the optimal mix of cash, bonds, stocks and

PEARLS OF WISDOM

Few things are more expensive than stretching for extra yield.

other assets that create the best long-term results and let us sleep well at night. One thing is for certain in the nest egg design business: Everyone is different!

Young investors, for example, should have a much longer time horizon and a higher risk tolerance for building their nest eggs than a new retiree. Consequently, a young investor's mix of investments could tolerate more risk (a higher overall Beta perhaps) for the possibility of greater growth potential.

As Ben Graham might say, younger investors can afford to be more "enterprising." It is important to note, however, that growth is never guaranteed even though you start the nest egg building plan very early.

Most investors assume that if you continually invest in a mix of high quality bonds and stocks throughout your life, you are virtually guaranteed that your nest egg will grow and beat the rate of inflation. While this is generally true, it is important to note that, over the past 100 years, there have been several lengthy and extremely painful periods in stock market history that have not produced positive returns even though investors followed the prudent diversification and timing rules.

You must be willing to develop staying power during these downturns in markets and not sell out. We will discuss these negative return periods in detail in Chapter 4, "Stocks for the Long Run," and how to navigate and endure them.

How Many Asset Categories Do You Need?

There has always been a debate in academia about how many individual investment or asset categories are needed for one to diversify risk. What would that look like? Well, for example, if one of your asset types were to decline in value, other classes should be in place that move in the opposite direction and create a hedge.

Thousands of studies have been conducted with a variety of outcomes. I believe that between six and 10 investment categories have performed best over time for our nest egg.

If you divide 6 or 10 into 100, you will see that your maximum investment in any one category, if they are all equally divided, will be between 10 and 17 percent. That feels about right to me. I always make sure that no single investment in anything can ever devastate our nest egg. It is always possible to eliminate or switch any individual investment class if something dramatic happens, like a change in tax laws, for instance.

I think three investment categories, while simple and easy to manage, is too few, and 25 is too many. You can explore the large body of research and literature on this subject on the Internet. It is very interesting and there is mathematical support for different combinations of investments and numbers of categories.

Vanguard recently explored the various returns resulting from alternating the mix of stocks versus bonds over history. As you can see from the chart, more volatility has generally meant more return and less volatility, lower returns. This makes sense.

WITH BONDS, LESS VOLATILITY BUT LOWER RETURNS

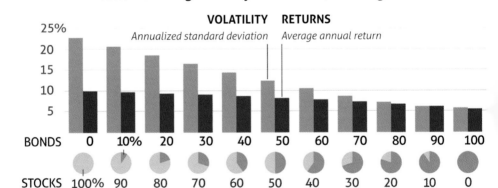

Historical average volatility and returns 1926 through 2011

A Vanguard study of the historic returns of stocks and bonds found that as a portfolio is weighted more heavily with bonds, the portfolio's returns are a bit lower, but when it's weighted more heavily with stock, it's much more volatile.

It was intriguing for me to see that a 50-50 stock-bond allocation, over time, has produced roughly 8 percent returns with about 12 percent price volatility. By contrast, portfolios invested 100 percent in stocks have produced only 2 percent more in annual returns but market volatility almost doubles! This research makes a strong case for keeping your stock and bond percentages relatively equal. Also, it keeps things simple and easy to manage.

You can see below how the Goble nest egg is currently diversified. I spend most of my strategy time looking at the performance of each asset class and thinking about whether the percentages are correct given what is happening in the markets and the world. There is certainly no right or wrong breakdown. Everyone should create their own mix based on a variety of market and life factors. I enjoy reviewing these reports each month.

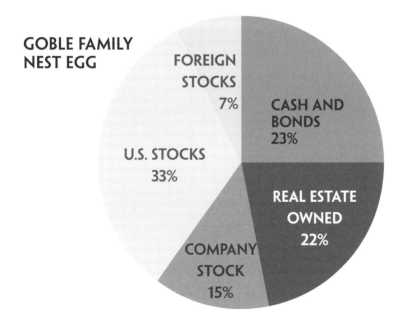

GOBLE FAMILY NEST EGG

FOREIGN STOCKS 7%

CASH AND BONDS 23%

U.S. STOCKS 33%

REAL ESTATE OWNED 22%

COMPANY STOCK 15%

At the time of this writing, the Dow Jones Industrial Average is about 18000, an all-time high. I frequently ask myself, "What is doing the best now?" Then, "What is most out of favor?"

Should I pull a little out of the "popular" classes (stocks, at present) and reinvest into the "out of favor" classes (currently cash or bonds)? I usually make these adjustments in several, small incremental moves. I think of these mix adjustments as if they were small brush strokes in a larger painting. We'll go deeper into this rebalancing process in Chapter 7.

Howard Marks often poses another interesting question to his team: "What is the biggest investing mistake we can possibly make right now?"

This question can often uncover concentrations or particular sectors that will not likely contribute to Alpha, and can be a very healthy practice for thinking outside the box. It also helps one reduce the downside exposure to the markets.

For instance, although very tempting during a time of record stock prices, adding significant new dollars to this highest priced investment class could be the "biggest mistake" now. It is always more tempting to add cash to classes that are rising in price rather than falling, but one has to remember the countercyclical mantra.

Required Homework

I personally love to read to stay current. We subscribe to the New York Times, The Kansas City Star, USA Today, The Wall Street Journal and Barron's. They are all delivered to our home and I often meet our paper delivery person at the end of our driveway at 6 a.m. With regard to this ritual, my wife Sharon often kids me that I need to get out more; I know it's a little compulsive. I can't wait to see what news has occurred each day.

I also have seven (my lucky number) years of daily activities recorded in a day planner, so I can tell you quickly where I was and what I was doing on any day over the last seven years. A horseshoe on the wall in my office at the bank points upward for good investment luck. As Sharon says, I need to get out more.

I like the business sections of The New York Times and USA Today. They are well written and concise. The Times, especially, has a robust graphics staff that makes great charts and illustrations. They quickly cut to the chase. My favorites are the Money section of USA Today and the Sunday Business section of the Times. I always learn something new or a new way of thinking about or presenting a topic.

I enjoy reading the paper versions of these newspapers (rather than online) and I read them in exactly the same order every day. It's ok if you think this is a little too structured. It is my routine and it works for me.

Academic studies have shown that a very high percentage (I have seen numbers as high as 90 percent) of your success in growing your nest egg relates to the attention you give to creating the proper mix of investments each year and avoiding single concentrations that could create very bad financial events.

That's important enough to discuss in a little more depth. Let me start with a personal example.

Company Stock?

One thing that stands out in our nest egg chart on page 27 is the concentration in a single stock: UMB Financial Corp (UMBF). At present, we have about 15 percent invested in company stock. I monitor this concentration and try to reduce it when possible to mitigate our overall "bad event" risk.

Next year will be my 35th at UMB. I have purchased shares of UMBF every year so it has accumulated into a large percentage of our nest egg over my career. In general, although our stock has appreciated nicely over the years, it is never prudent from a diversification perspective to hold too much of one thing.

We liquidate UMBF shares from time to time to reduce this exposure when it becomes too large. I realize that there is a price to this rebalancing with a stock that has appreciated steadily, but it is something I believe in for nest egg safety's sake.

PEARLS OF WISDOM

When prices are falling you must have discipline to keep investing. Don't be sore, buy some more.

There are many, many stories of employees losing nearly everything when their formerly solid employer suddenly filed for bankruptcy or otherwise had its stock price plummet or collapse. Several of these collapses occurred in companies with long histories of success (Enron and Lehman Brothers come to mind), but something suddenly changed or they made poor choices that eventually cost them their company, and their nest eggs.

I know several people who have had to either start over or extend their working careers past normal retirement age due to these life-changing unpredictable stock market events. The potential gain of significantly overweighting your company's stock in your nest egg is simply not worth the potential pain, in my opinion.

Obviously, I have a lot of faith in UMB's management and board of directors that this could never happen to the firm, but I still think it makes sense to not bet my entire nest egg on any one company. UMB's management understands this risk for its lifetime employees. They allow us to liquidate shares as we reach age benchmarks.

My goal for our nest egg is simply to have it grow consistently and safely, hopefully with positive Alpha each year. I also subscribe to Howard Mark's strategy that it is ok to accept a little less Alpha each year in return for avoiding serious losses when markets turn sharply lower. We plan for the worst, but hope for the best.

The powerful surge in stock prices in recent years has been a great thing, but I also remember 2008-2009, when the stock market was struggling over the real estate meltdown and Lehman Brothers' collapse on Wall Street. Lehman Brothers was a 146-year-old investment-banking firm. Just think of the losses Lehman employees had if they owned only or mostly Lehman stock.

On March 9, 2009, the Dow Jones Industrial Average bottomed out at 6547, down 54 percent (or over 7600 points) from the previous high set on Oct. 9, 2007.

PEARLS OF WISDOM

Never let your past dictate who you are...but let it help you become who you might be.

STOCK DROPS AND RECOVERIES

Dow Jones Industrials
2000 - Current

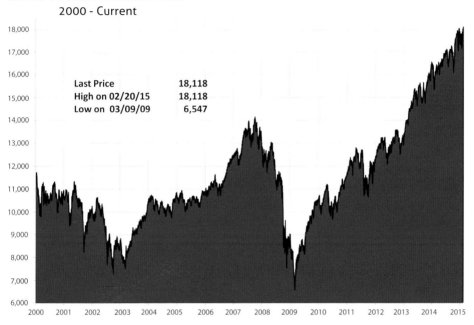

Last Price	18,118
High on 02/20/15	18,118
Low on 03/09/09	6,547

I actually followed the countercyclical formula and sold bonds to add money to our stock funds in several stages near the bottom. That has worked out very well for us so far. I cannot say it was without a little trepidation and queasiness that we made changes in our percentage allocation, but I knew what the great investors in Chapter 2 would have suggested in the middle of such historic market turmoil. You can see how it looked in the chart above.

You have to stay objective and fight off the negative emotions, as these drops in the market often accompany great investing opportunities. A queasy stomach, I have found, can be a very strong indicator that there are great opportunities for Alpha. You must be willing to do the opposite of what you would like to do at the time to protect your nest egg!

While diversification is clearly one of the most basic tenets of success-ful investing, it is possible to be too diversified, that is, holding too many individual classes of investments, which can actually dampen or reduce your performance and really not lower your overall risk profile.

I have never been a fan of owning gold or annuities, for example, but that is a personal choice for every investor. You may feel differently and that is fine as your nest egg needs to be a reflection of you, not someone else.

A Diversification Formula

In a perfect investing world, your mix of investments will always complement one another, market conditions, and your stage in life. I have developed a formula to help gauge that, which has worked well for our nest egg and I hope might be of some benefit to you.

It takes into consideration only the "safe" parts of your nest egg – so stocks aren't included and, to compensate for market swings, only 75 percent of your home value.

The underlying principle is that you should keep approximately your age in safe stuff. If you are 20, risk is welcomed at 80 percent. At 90, only 10 percent is advised.

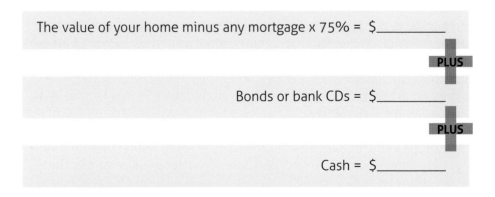

The value of your home minus any mortgage x 75% = $_____

PLUS

Bonds or bank CDs = $_____

PLUS

Cash = $_____

Next, divide the dollar amount in each category by your net worth or nest egg total.

Convert each of the three categories to a percent of the total in your nest egg and then add them up.

The total should approximate your age. If it doesn't, you might want to consider increasing the amount of your nest egg held in safe investments. It also might show that you can perhaps afford to take more risk, when the time is right.

In my opinion, paying attention to diversification is the number one practice that leads, over time, to building a successful nest egg.

Here is my list of the five most important investment considerations, in order of importance:

1   Diversification of nest egg (no excessive concentrations)
2   Quality and prudent terms of investments selected
3   Timing of rebalances each year
4   Discipline of automated monthly investment
5   Attention to your plan

Next, in Chapters 4 and 5 we will begin a study of the importance of owning stocks and bonds and how they should be selected.

NEST EGG

CHAPTER
FOUR

STOCKS FOR
THE LONG RUN

Stocks have outperformed every other asset since 1802.

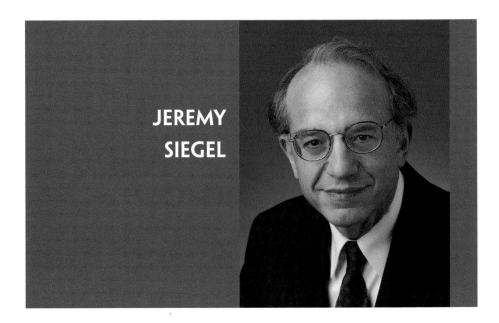

JEREMY
SIEGEL

Good Guidance

Jeremy Siegel is one of my favorite stock market experts for three reasons: He takes a long-term view of the market, he loves history, and most importantly, he is an optimist about America's future.

I would love to meet him someday.

He reminds me of my favorite MBA Finance Professor at the University of Kansas, Dr. Maurice Joy. Unlike many Wall Street types, Siegel seems calm, confident and very professor-like when he speaks or is interviewed. There is no sales pitch.

He is currently the Russell E. Palmer Professor of Finance at the University of Pennsylvania's Wharton School of Finance, one of the leading business schools in the nation. His undergraduate degree is from Columbia University in New York and he holds a Ph.D. from Boston's Massachusetts Institute of Technology. Those are fabulous credentials.

Siegel's classic 1994 book, "Stocks for the Long Run," is another must read for investors looking for more knowledge and perspective about the market. His nickname is the "Wizard of Wharton," and I love watching his interviews on TV.

The book's subtitle is "The Definitive Guide to Financial Market Returns and Long-Term Investment Strategies." The Washington Post called it "one of the 10 best investment books of all time," well-deserved praise.

Now in its 5th edition, it's 403 pages, so you may wish to make it one of your nightstand books. However, it's a fun and interesting read and is filled with great stock market history, charts and graphs, as well as valuable guidance.

Since professionally I only work with municipal and government bonds, reading Siegel's book was an excellent way to learn more in a very short time about the history of the stock market. I took notes.

In the introduction, Siegel makes a statement about the stock market with which I agree: "Although...returns may be diminished from the past, there is overwhelming reason to believe stocks will remain the best investment for all those seeking steady, long-term gains."

I share his optimistic view that the stock market generally reflects the high degree of faith we as Americans have in our future. While there will most certainly be periods of excess, extreme volatility and falling prices (reference the 46 percent stock market collapse in 2008-2009), I believe that over the long run, when we buy stocks of great companies, we are investing in the future and success of America. On that, I am very bullish.

Of course that is not to say that all of your nest egg should be in stocks.

One Man's Prediction

I saw a March 2014 CNBC interview with Warren Buffett in which he talked about his penchant for investing in great American companies that he fully understands. And, he made a few predictions.

He said he thought the Dow Jones Industrial Average, currently hovering around its all-time high of 18000, would someday hit 20000, 50000 and perhaps even 100000, although probably not in his lifetime.

Even more interesting, he said it was very likely that the market would be cut in half several times during this climb. Volatility is part of the long-term market pricing process because the market is a discounting mechanism for future events, and world events can be very uncertain at times.

Siegel points out that poorly underwritten home mortgages were the main culprit in the Great Recession of 2008-2009. This was different from the excessive speculation in stocks that greatly contributed to the 1929 Great Depression market crash. In both market collapses, there were many other contributing factors.

One thing is for sure. In all of our major market corrections, you can count on the pendulum of greed and fear having swung too far in one direction. Bull markets (long periods of rising stock prices) generally do not simply die of old age. Some extraneous event usually triggers the end of a rally in stock prices. The market has recovered each time, as Buffett predicted, but there is no 100 percent guarantee that this will be true in the future.

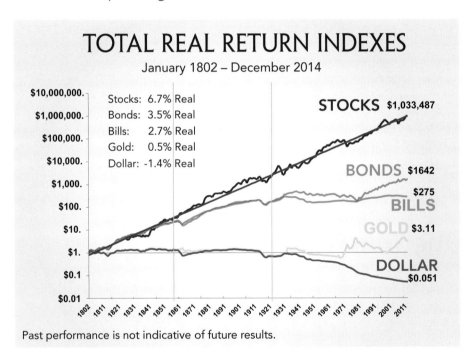

TOTAL REAL RETURN INDEXES
January 1802 – December 2014

Stocks: 6.7% Real
Bonds: 3.5% Real
Bills: 2.7% Real
Gold: 0.5% Real
Dollar: -1.4% Real

STOCKS $1,033,487

BONDS $1642

$275

BILLS

GOLD $3.11

DOLLAR

$0.051

Past performance is not indicative of future results.

The chart above is from "Stocks for the Long Run." It shows that stocks have outperformed every other major asset class since 1802. In his book, Siegel cites historical market evidence to show how well stocks have performed long term and contends that the volatility one experiences from time to time, although sometimes unsettling, will most likely be worth it.

Indeed, he says that stocks over long time horizons are actually less volatile than bonds, which I found interesting. You also can see in the chart how the U.S. dollar has devalued over the years. Siegel's research shows a 1.4 percent loss in purchasing power each year since 1802.

As of this writing, however, the dollar is recovering sharply versus other major global currencies, having risen about 10 percent for the year. All of a sudden, the U.S. economy appears to be once again the strongest in the world, as Europe, China, Japan and Russia are all facing serious recessionary pressures from falling oil prices and fears of deflation.

There have been many sharp declines in stock market history. You can see when these periods were and the depth of the market downturn in the chart below.

DOW JONES INDUSTRIAL AVERAGE: TOP 10 LARGEST DAILY PERCENTAGE LOSSES

Rank	Date	Close	Net Change	% Change
1	10-19-1987	1,738.74	-508.00	-22.61
2	10-28-1929	260.64	-38.33	-12.82
3	10-29-1929	230.07	-30.57	-11.73
4	11-06-1929	232.13	-25.55	-9.92
5	12-18-1899	58.27	-5.57	-8.72
6	08-12-1932	63.11	-5.79	-8.40
7	03-14-1907	76.23	-6.89	-8.29
8	10-26-1987	1,793.93	-156.83	-8.04
9	10-15-2008	8,577.91	-733.08	-7.87
10	07-21-1933	88.71	-7.55	-7.84

Intelligent investors know that these periods of market volatility and negative returns are likely and are prepared to preserve their nest egg and not panic. They are able to see the corrections as great opportunities for the future growth of their nest eggs. I will discuss this in greater depth in Chapter 7.

The Great Recession Of 2008-2009

At the time of this writing, the U.S. economy is digging out of its deepest economic downturn since the Great Depression, almost 90 years ago. At the core of our most recent economic collapse was wild speculation in commercial and residential real estate.

That stage was followed by trillions of dollars invested globally in questionable American home mortgages whose AAA ratings by professional ratings agencies now appear to have greatly misrepresented their intrinsic quality. Many people who could barely afford one home . . . owned several.

It was a bubble in home mortgage lending of such magnitude that it nearly triggered a global financial meltdown. This is the definition of the greed pendulum swinging too far. You can see in the chart below from "Stocks for the Long Run" by Jeremy Siegel how real estate values were way off of their normal relationship to personal income, which should have been a strong warning signal.

A BUBBLE THAT BURST

The market value of housing relative to the national income average.

The Federal Reserve System, under Chairman Ben Bernanke, had no choice but to take historic, unprecedented action. It embarked on three rounds of market stimulus referred to now as "quantitative easing," or QE. I think of QE as adrenalin for a patient in cardiac arrest.

Those three rounds of bond buying resulted in the Fed's bond holdings swelling to over $4 trillion, over eight times its normal size. You can see the Fed's portfolio at present below, as well as its rapid expansion in size.

THE FED'S BOND PORTFOLIO

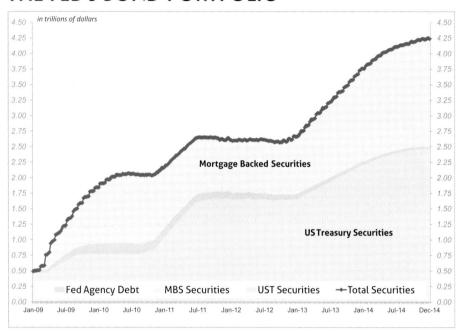

There is always controversy when our Treasury and Federal Reserve intervene to effectively bail out companies (or our economy), but they simply had no choice. The potential damage to both the domestic and global economies was too great. It probably would have been severe enough to create another Great Depression, so historic measures, controversial as they were, were required.

Chairman Bernanke, one of the world's great experts on deflation and the Great Depression, was the perfect man to lead the Federal Reserve during this global financial crisis. If you are interested in reading more on this subject, Bernanke's book, "Essays on the Great Depression," is an excellent historical read on the most perilous economic period in American history.

I have never met Ben Bernanke but have been fortunate to meet former Federal Reserve chairmen Alan Greenspan and Paul Volcker. If I ever meet Bernanke, and I'd love to, I'd thank him. I think he is a patriot.

His book gave me great perspective about how horrible financial conditions were in the 1930s. There were many scenes, such as the one below, of men in business suits waiting for food in bread lines as the unemployment rate hit 23.6 percent in 1932. The Hoover Dam, Golden Gate Bridge and the Empire State Building are all iconic national construction projects that were completed to help create jobs during the Great Depression.

TWO HISTORIC DOWNTURNS

	1929-1933	2008
Dow Jones Average Low (% loss)	33 (90%)	8,175 (40%)
Interest rates	Rising sharply	Falling sharply
Bank deposit insurance	Did not exist	$250 k (12/09)
Bank failures	1,200	465 (2008-2012)
Unemployment insurance	Did not exist	States set rules
Unemployment rate peak	25%	6.1% (and rising)

As of this writing, the economy has improved from the recession of 2008-2009, the unemployment rate has fallen below 6 percent, and it appears that the Federal Reserve is planning to gradually reduce the size of its bond portfolio and the scope of QE.

There has been much discussion about the timing of the exit plan. Janet Yellen has succeeded Ben Bernanke as chairman of the Fed.

Ms. Yellen is very qualified to lead the Fed. Her credentials are impeccable. She has a Ph.D. in economics from Yale and an undergraduate degree (summa cum laude) in economics from Brown University.

Her mentor was, after all, Ben Bernanke. She is the first woman to hold the position and is building credibility and trust with Wall Street and politicians in Washington as well. This will take some time, but she is credible and forthcoming.

Janet Yellen

Did You Know?

It's often been said that while market history may not repeat itself exactly...it often rhymes. The Stock Traders Almanac is another excellent reference source on the historical and sometimes quirky trends in the market. Each year, Jeffrey and Yale Hirsch provide an updated version of the trends and tendencies they follow. Their research is fascinating, fun and educational. I also believe that some of their predictions become self-fulfilling prophecies because the media covers them in great detail.

Here are some of my favorite stock market fun facts from the 2015 (48th edition) of the Almanac:

- The year before a presidential election is far and away the best year of the presidential cycle, averaging a positive 16 percent return each time since 1938.

- Years ending in a five have averaged a 28.3 percent return since 1885.

- Since 1955, April has been the best month for the Dow.

- November and December rank number two and three, respectively, because of the frequent occurrence of a "Santa Claus rally" at the end of the year.

- The performance of the market in early January, also known as the "January effect," has correctly predicted the direction of the markets for the entire year in 14 of the last 16 years.

- Fridays and Mondays are the most important stock trading days of the week. Mondays factor in all of the weekend news and Fridays are position-balancing days before the weekend.

And finally:

- The 2015 Almanac has updated its forecast for the Dow Jones Average in 2025 to be 38820.

Conclusion: 'Stocks Will Fluctuate'

When asked in October 1922 what one should expect from the stock market going forward, New York banker J.P. Morgan said, with a wink, "Stocks will fluctuate."

I believe stocks should be considered for the long run. Like many things in life, one needs to build a level of comfort about the stock market, and that comfort level usually begins with knowledge. I am convinced, after all of my research and personal experience investing in the market, that stocks provide the best chance for most of us to successfully grow our nest eggs into something extraordinary.

In Chapter 5, we will look at how bonds can provide the bedrock for steady returns, a hedge for your nest egg and also a way for you to invest in stocks when market opportunities arise, as they undoubtedly will.

PEARLS OF WISDOM

No pain, no gain. Good long-term investments can often make you a little queasy at first.

NEST EGG

PRESERVING YOUR NEST EGG WITH BONDS

Bonds and cash can cushion your portfolio's volatility.

You're the Lender

I have been studying, writing and teaching about and working with bonds for more than 35 years. There remains much to learn in my opinion.

A bond is basically a financial promise or I.O.U. that requires the issuer to make regular interest payments over time to you, the bondholder. These payments also are known as "coupons."

You are effectively making a loan to the issuer of the bond. The borrower, in return, typically sends you interest payments twice a year. At the bond's maturity date, you get back your initial loan (the principal) plus the last interest payment.

In the distant past, a paper coupon was physically attached to each bond and the bondholder would "clip" it off the bond with scissors and present it to a bank or paying agent for payment. You also could mail the coupon in for collection.

That's why, historically, banks have hung a pair of scissors in the vault for the use of customers visiting their safety deposit boxes.

Coupon Clippers?

Hence, another name for conservative investors who hold bonds in their nest eggs is "coupon clippers." Today, almost all bonds exist in book-entry or electronic form, ending the need for clipping.

Once you buy a bond, your interest payments are fixed at a specific rate, as is the amount of time for which you will receive the payments, called the term of the bond. That's why bonds are often called "fixed" income.

Stocks, on the other hand, are often called "equities" because you actually own an equity portion of the company. Some companies make quarterly payments to shareholders, but these are called dividends, not interest payments, and are typically based on sharing the company's profits with its shareholders. Stock dividends can be changed each year by management based on the company's performance.

I think of bonds generally in two components: the semiannual interest payments, and the final return of your principal at the bond's maturity.

I visualize the interest payments on a time line as I attempt to stagger the cash flows in a portfolio of bonds. A bond due in September, for example, will pay interest each March and September. A bond due in July will pay interest each January and again six months later in July. You get the picture.

If market interest rates could remain perfectly constant during the period you hold the bond, the market value of your bond would never change. This, of course, never happens! Like the stock market, prices in the bond market are always changing and unpredictable.

Your bond's price, if you were buying or selling it today, will move up and down daily with the market. This only matters to you if you sell your bond before its maturity date. More on that later.

In fact, Ben Graham's rules about how investors often waste too much time and effort trying to outguess the stock market, also apply to the bond market. Even after 35 years of investing in bonds, I am still unsure about the bond market's future direction at any given time.

SIZE OF BOND MARKET VS SIZE OF STOCK MARKET

$37 trillion

$21 trillion

The U.S. bond market is roughly 43 percent larger than the stock market, making it easily the largest and most liquid financial market in the world.

On its maturity date, a bond's price always returns to exactly 100 cents on the dollar that you paid for it. That's called its "par" value. This return of all your principal is the beauty of bonds, and the obvious reason for their popularity for nest egg building.

If you invest in FDIC-insured certificates of deposit from banks and very low risk bonds like those backed by the U.S. government or its agencies, you are essentially 100 percent assured of always receiving all your investment back. This is the basis for the investment adage that says stocks can make you rich and safe bonds can keep you rich.

Bonds, along with your cash position, can often act as a stabilizing or balancing force for your stock portfolio. Bond and stock prices generally move in opposite directions so there is often a built-in counterbalance, or hedge, between the two asset classes. It is not a perfect hedge, of course. (So far, I have only found one of those, in Tokyo.)

The author found one perfect hedge, near the Imperial Palace in Japan.

This inverse relationship is the basis for why investors should always hold both stocks and bonds in a proportion that best suits one's age and risk tolerance.

You may remember that in Chapter 3 I reviewed the performance of various stock/bond allocations over time, and that 50/50 or 60/40 stock/bond blends both appear to create a good balance with better than average returns...and lower price swings.

Teeter-Totter?

One mental image that can help investors understand the inverse mechanics of bonds is that of a teeter-totter, those pieces of equipment that used to be seen on school playgrounds. In the market, as bond prices rise, their interest rates, also called yields, will fall, and vice versa.

Throughout the life of a bond, the teeter-totter will move up and down as your bond's market value is constantly adjusted to changes in the current bond market. Every day, your current holdings are effectively re-priced or "marked to the market," and so they will fluctuate in price until the bond reaches maturity.

If you need to sell a bond before its maturity date, you are subject to the market price that day, which may be higher or lower than your original purchase price. This is how bond gains and losses are created, and they can often be used to offset gains or losses you may have from stocks or real estate. Banks, for example, usually have very large bond portfolios and often execute trades to create gains or losses according to their strategy.

At maturity, your original principal is returned whole, and you can spend it, invest it in the stock market, or in a new bond. In the meantime, you have collected semiannual interest payments to be spent or saved for future reinvestment.

Unlike the stock market, the likelihood of receiving regular interest pay-ments, and 100 percent of your principal investment back, is comforting for bond investors, especially those who are risk averse, or whose main goal is to maintain their nest egg.

I'm interested in coins and find it intriguing why bonds are priced in eighths (and sometimes 32nds) of 1 percent. The tradition ties to the American colonies, where the main currency was the Spanish dollar coin. Made of silver, it was worth eight reales and could be physically broken into eight pieces to make change – thus the term pieces of eight (in Spanish, peso de ocho). Stocks also were priced in 32nds but have since switched to decimals.

Spanish coins also figure in the creation of the American dollar sign ($), which actually is a peso sign. The abbreviation for the Spanish peso, was PS. Merchants saved time by writing the "P" and "S" on top of each other. Eventually, they dropped the bowl from the "P" entirely and thus was born the peso sign ($). Because the U.S. dollar was named after the Spanish peso de ocho "dollar" coin, the peso symbol was ultimately used to refer to pesos and dollars both.

Above, two Spanish silver pieces of eight.

Right, a silver Spanish dollar coin from 1789. The purpose of the serrated edge was to prevent shaving silver off of the coin. This was America's first coin.

Building A Bond Ladder

In the safety portion of your investment plan, high quality bonds (and FDIC-insured bank CDs) should be the backbone. Holding a portion of your nest egg in cash also has always been wise.

Although never as exciting as their stock and stock mutual fund cousins, bonds and bond mutual funds play a critical role in many wealthy investors' nest eggs. They provide constant income whether times are good or bad. They allow risk to be more carefully focused elsewhere in your nest egg plan. The income earned can even be tax free if you choose a qualifying bond.

Over the years, I have worked with many wealthy investors who own no stocks or stock mutual funds at all!

After a lifetime of working and saving, why, they ask, would they risk losing even a penny of their hard earned nest egg to the unpredictable and volatile stock market? This is a choice they make and it helps them enjoy life and sleep better, and that is really what's important.

They point out that over one particular 10-year period of investing in the stock market (1999-2009) they would basically have not earned a single penny. Point well taken. There have been many other periods where positive returns were not achieved. The stock market, as we have discussed, does not have a risk-free guarantee. We will discuss this in depth in Chapter 8.

If you happen to be at a similar stage in your life and nest egg building process or if you share this very conservative view, laddering maturities of bonds and certificates of deposit is a safe and predictable way to preserve your nest egg. There are a few tricks to the trade, however.

How It Works

Laddering bonds is a technique of staggering the maturity dates of bonds so you have cash coming in from monthly, quarterly or semiannual interest and principal payments at all times throughout the year. You can see a simplified illustration below.

You are creating a steady cash flow stream either for living expenses or regular reinvestment in your nest egg. Regular investment helps one participate in all markets, if desired, which often boosts performance.

LADDERING BONDS BY MATURITIES

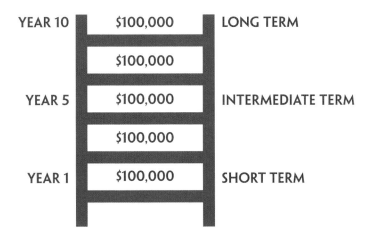

YEAR 10	$100,000	LONG TERM
	$100,000	
YEAR 5	$100,000	INTERMEDIATE TERM
	$100,000	
YEAR 1	$100,000	SHORT TERM

I work with many banks on their bond portfolios and it is not uncommon for a bank to hold hundreds of millions of dollars in very safe bonds.

Banks use the regular cash flow of interest and principal payments each month to then make loans, fund deposit withdrawals or purchase new bonds. We use our bond portfolio for liquidity first, and yield second.

My first book, "More Yield, Less Risk... Better Sleep!" was written for bank bond portfolio managers . Because of their role in protecting deposits with FDIC insurance, banks, by law, cannot own common stocks in their portfolios, with a very few exceptions.

A simple yet effective bond laddering strategy is to first purchase a series of bonds that mature monthly or quarterly over the next few years. If you receive a lump sum of cash from a retirement fund or the sale of your business, this is a good way to start.

As time passes and bonds mature from your ladder, you may:

1   Use the cash for living expenses or something fun
2   Reinvest the cash in a new bond
3   Reinvest the cash in the stock market
4   Hold the cash in reserve

Dollar Cost Averaging and Bonds

Basically, your overall investment goal in purchasing either stocks or bonds is to "buy low and sell high." Whenever a bond pays interest or principal, you are searching the markets for the optimum opportunity to reinvest and increase your nest egg's overall performance. If you decide to reinvest in your bond ladder, a good rule of thumb is to purchase shorter-term bonds for your ladder when their yield is lower than your portfolio's overall average yield.

If the yield on your new bond is higher than your overall average yield, you should purchase a bond that is generally longer than the average maturity of the bonds in your portfolio. This technique is called dollar cost averaging, and it works for both stocks and bonds. You are trying to effectively lower your average cost basis each time you invest, which increases your overall returns (or Alpha).

The Barbell Technique

Another option to consider when investing in bonds is called the barbell technique. It graphs out with a distribution shaped like a weight lifter's barbell. This technique suggests that investors hold more short-term bonds than they would in a perfectly uniform ladder and more long-term bonds at the same time, as well.

Similar to the dollar cost averaging strategy, you would purchase shorter-term bonds for your barbell when your new bond's yield is less than your portfolio's overall average yield.

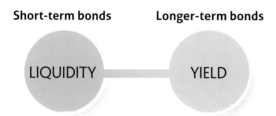

Short-term bonds   **Longer-term bonds**

LIQUIDITY   YIELD

As with a bond ladder, you should purchase longer-term bonds for your barbell strategy when they improve the overall average of your portfolio. There are fewer bond maturities scheduled in the middle years using this hedging strategy.

For many investors, longer term, high quality tax-free bonds are an excellent option. I will discuss their advantages in Chapter 6.

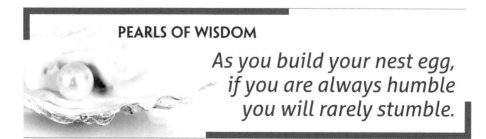

PEARLS OF WISDOM

As you build your nest egg, if you are always humble you will rarely stumble.

The Ski Jump

The final portfolio design technique is one I developed and call the "ski jump strategy" because of its similarity to the winter Olympics sport. In some ways, it combines the ladder and barbell strategies, and optimizes both.

Since 1979, interest rates have basically been falling and currently are at some of the lowest levels in history, partly due to the Federal Reserve's quantitative easing programs.

PORTFOLIO CASH FLOW ANALYSIS

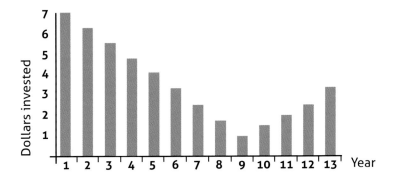

If you were lucky enough to have been investing in bonds in the late 1970s and early 1980s, you were able to earn double-digit returns. I remember the Prime Lending Rate for banks peaking at 21.5 percent and longer term bonds that yielded more than 15 percent. I think it is a pretty safe bet that we will never see those yields again!

In the chart on the next page, note the Federal Reserve chairmen listed across the bottom, the last being Janet Yellen, the new Fed chair.

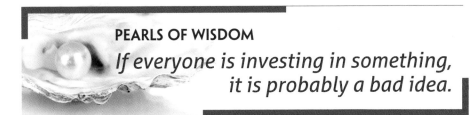

PEARLS OF WISDOM

If everyone is investing in something, it is probably a bad idea.

INTEREST RATES   THE BIG PICTURE

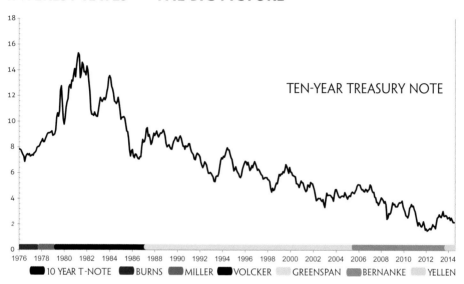

TEN-YEAR TREASURY NOTE

10 Year Treasurey Note Yield   1976-Present

Key Bond Terms To Know

Par   The face dollar amount of your bond.

Principal amount Original cost of your bond, including premium or discount amount.

Coupon rate   The annual rate of interest you will be paid.

Premium   The amount you must pay over the par amount in order to purchase a larger coupon rate than your bond's yield to maturity.

Discount   The amount under par you must pay for a bond to compensate you for a coupon rate less than your bond's yield to maturity.

Amortization	The regular reduction in your bond's principal cost when purchased at a premium so that your bond can mature at par.
Accretion	The regular increase in your bond's principal cost when purchased at a discount so that your bond can mature at par.
Yield to maturity/call	The effective yield of your bond assuming that all interest payments are reinvested at the bond's yield on its original purchase date.
Total Return	The sum of a bond's yield to maturity and any gains or losses due to changes in the price of your bond while you own it.
Average Maturity	The weighted average time in years to the maturity of your bond.
Duration	The price sensitivity of your bond as a percentage given its coupon rate and maturity given a 1 percent change in interest rates.
Convexity	The ability of a bond to hold its market value as interest rates go up and down.

For those who enjoy math, I thought you might appreciate learning more about how bonds with different coupon rates perform in the market, given changes in interest rates. You can see in the chart on the next page how different coupon rates can affect the overall performance of a bond.

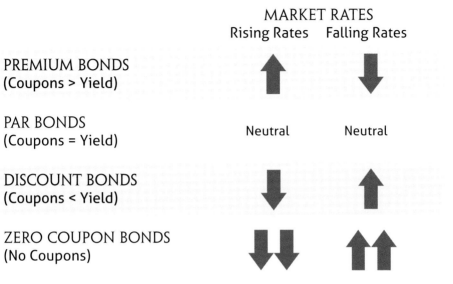

	MARKET RATES	
PREMIUM BONDS (Coupons > Yield)	Rising Rates	Falling Rates
PAR BONDS (Coupons = Yield)	Neutral	Neutral
DISCOUNT BONDS (Coupons < Yield)		
ZERO COUPON BONDS (No Coupons)		

Market performance is determined in terms of bond prices, not yield.

Conclusions

Bonds are a very important part of one's nest egg, whether you invest in individual bonds, CDs or bond mutual funds. They can provide an important source of regular income as well as a stabilizing force, or hedge, for one's stock portfolio. They, along with cash, are the safety valve for your nest egg. As Ben Graham reminds us, you should always have at least 25 percent of your nest egg in cash and bonds.

The percentage of bonds or CDs one owns relates to the factors I have been discussing and certainly will vary with each investor. Hopefully, you now have a better level of comfort with how bonds work and the benefits of laddering or staggering maturities.

I will now explore tax-free bonds and their nest egg benefits.

NEST EGG

HOW TO SELECT MUNICIPAL BONDS FOR YOUR NEST EGG

The appeal of municipal bonds is that they can be tax free.

Still A Tax Shelter

In the safety net portion of your nest egg, tax-free bonds, also known as municipal bonds, make solid and predictable investments for many investors.

Because these bonds produce income that can be exempt from local, state and federal taxes, they are excellent investment tools for building and preserving wealth. They are popular for individual and bank/institutional investors because they have predictable, tax-free returns of principal.

Many investors want to know what yield they would need to get on a taxable bond to equal their tax-free bond's yield. That is called the tax equivalent yield. Below is the formula for figuring it.

The tax-free bond's yield	2.0%
Divided by the number 1 minus your tax bracket (.34 for example)	(1– .34=.66)
Equals the tax equivalent yield	**3.03%**

There are several types of municipal bonds, also referred to in the industry as "munis."

General Obligation Bonds

This is a category of municipal bonds backed by the full taxing authority of the issuer. Issuers are generally cities, counties, states and school districts in the U.S. General obligation bonds are widely regarded as the safest of municipal bonds and are backed by "ad valorem," or unlimited property tax assessment authority.

In other words, if something should harm a municipal bond's underlying financial condition, the issuer has the legal authority to raise property taxes on the residents of the municipality without limit until the bond is paid off in full. Consequently, the overall historical default rate for general obligation bonds is very low.

Revenue Bonds

Revenue bonds are munis issued by municipalities to finance specific revenue-producing projects. In contrast to general obligations, revenue bonds rely solely on the success of the project to repay investors. They come with no property tax assessment taxing authority. A very common revenue bond is one used by states to pay for interstate highways. In that case, the toll one pays to use the toll road directly pays off the bonds.

Other types of "essential purpose" revenue bonds include those to finance water, sewer and other public utilities. For the investor, the more essential the better.

US Treasury Notes	$138,000,000
Agency Bonds	$511,493,875
Mortgage-backed Pools	$431,258,000
Collateralized Mortgage Obligations (CMOs)	$319,668,616
Municipal Bonds:	$1,400,420,560
Total:	$2,800,841,051

As you can see from the chart above, of $2.8 billion in bond holdings, my personal clients on average own about 50 percent in tax-free municipal bonds, or $1.4 billion.

I'm using my personal clients as examples to show how wealthy people and institutions diversify and spread risk around. What's good for them may be good for you, too.

The value of municipal bonds over taxable alternatives has risen dramatically in the past several years because munis were not included in the Federal Reserve's quantitative easing bond buying programs. This made them attractive versus taxable bond investments for which the Fed has been pushing prices higher and yields lower.

Consequently, tax-free bonds have not fallen in yield as much as taxable investments. Investors have been buying more, or overweighting, the municipal bond asset class. I think this makes good sense, as long as the quality of the issues they hold is high and one keeps an eye on the dynamics of the Federal Reserve's plans for exiting its bond-buying program. This pricing trend could reverse at some point.

MUNI HOLDINGS AS OF 12-31-2014

PAR	TYPE
$1,340,053,383	General Obligation Municipal Bonds
$60,367,185	Revenue Bonds
$1,400,420,560	Total

You can see that approximately 95 percent of my clients' municipal bonds are general obligation bonds and that 4 percent are essential purpose (sewer, water and electricity) revenue bonds.

Rating Bonds

U.S. bonds are rated for their quality by two major agencies, Moody's Rating Service and Standard and Poors. The definitions of the quality ratings follow on the next page. The pie chart below that shows how my clients are currently invested per rating category.

Even though every investor should conduct her or his independent due diligence for the bond they are considering, a cross check is to regularly review their ratings. Most financial software packages include the monthly updated ratings of Moody's and/or Standard and Poors.

AAA Obligations rated Aaa are judged to be of the highest quality, subject to the lowest level of credit risk.

AA Obligations rated Aa are judged to be of high quality and are subject to very low credit risk.

A Obligations rated A are judged to be upper-medium grade and are subject to low credit risk.

BAA Obligations rated Baa are judged to be medium-grade and subject to moderate credit risk and as such may possess certain speculative characteristics.

BA Obligations rated Ba are judged to be speculative and are subject to substantial credit risk.

B Obligations rated B are considered speculative and are subject to high credit risk.

CAA Obligations rated Caa are judged to be speculative, of poor standing and are subject to very high credit risk.

CA Obligations rated Ca are highly speculative and are likely in, or very near, default, with some prospect of recovery of principal and interest.

C Obligations rated C are the lowest rated and are typically in default, with little prospect for recovery of principal or interest

RATING	PAR
AAA	$842,310,000
AA	$209,595,000
A	$249,025,000
BAA	$4,730,000
NR	$94,760,560
Total	$1, 400,420,560

Maximum Dollar Amount Per Bond?

Most investors set a maximum dollar amount that they can invest in any one municipality to diversify risk. This amount will vary with the size of your portfolio, but I have always thought that 2 to 3 percent is at least a target for a maximum dollar investment per issuer, unless the bonds are government guaranteed.

As mentioned earlier, federal and state taxes and sometimes even local taxes can be avoided by investing in the bonds of one's state of residency. It is prudent to diversify the types of your municipal holdings and their geography. In other words, avoid buying only school or city bonds issued by one school district or one city.

The Stay-Close-To-Home Rule

My rule for purchasing municipal bonds for clients is that, in general you should be able to drive there in a day or two to investigate anything negative that has surfaced about the financial condition of the municipality or school district. This regional investment rule of thumb also makes it more likely that you will hear or read about any changing financial condition before the bonds are affected. Below, the dollar amounts of my clients' municipal bond holdings by state. I realize it may be difficult to drive to Hawaii.

MUNIS BY STATE

IA	295,437,085	IL	64,621,100	WA	26,475,000
WI	222,214,993	PA	61,789,475	HI	19,235,000
MN	142,225,000	MO	53,177,000	AZ	18,525,000
TX	111,780,000	CO	39,755,000	SC	18,295,000
KS	86,972,800	SD	32,708,598	OR	16,810,000

MD	16,125,000	NJ	7,555,000	IN	1,800,000
OH	15,270,000	UT	7,015,000	NM	1,415,000
MI	14,755,000	NY	6,630,000	ME	1,355,000
NE	14,250,000	OK	6,390,000	DE	1,055,000
FL	12,965,000	AK	4,730,000	KY	800,000
VA	10,945,000	MA	4,420,000	ID	505,000
ND	10,248,949	AL	3,735,000	LA	335,000
TN	8,715,000	CA	3,680,000	AR	115,000
NC	8,695,000	RI	3,600,000	NH	100,000
GA	8,400,000	NV	3,490,000	**Total**	
CT	8,060,000	MS	2,825,000	**$1,400,420,560**	

Another Quality Check

A simple rule is to always purchase the highest quality bond you can find, even if the yield is less than others of lesser quality. I follow the adage that quality will always be there, long after the price is forgotten. I simply like to reduce the overall risk for our family nest egg and for my bond clients.

For even more due diligence, there are underwriting guidelines to help you (or your advisor) review the financial condition of the bond or bond fund you are considering. A few of the metrics I follow for both General Obligation and Revenue Bonds are listed on the next page.

PEARLS OF WISDOM

Generally speaking, if a certain investment grows too fast...it usually turns out to be a weed.

Well, you say, these charts may be vital tools for evaluating municipal bonds, but where does one get the data to complete them?

I, and many careful bond buyers, use EMMA, the Electronic Municipal Market Access website: www.emma.msrb.org. It provides free public access to information, including official disclosures, trade data and credit ratings on virtually all municipal securities.

GENERAL GUIDELINES FOR EVALUATING GENERAL OBLIGATION MUNICIPAL BONDS

Population	>	1,000	Local
	>	3,000	Regional
Direct Debt to Assessed Valuation *(depends on assessed value percentages as they vary from state to state)*	<	25%	
Direct Debt to Market Value	<	20%	
Direct Debt Per Capita	<	$4,000	
Overall Economic Condition		Stable	
Overall Financial Condition		Stable	
Tax Collections Last Three Years	>	95%+	
Top 10 Taxpayers Taxable Property as a % of Assessed Valuation	<	25%	
Concentration of Single Employer or Taxpayer		Absent	
Current Financial Statements Available (Audited)		Yes	
Reputation and Past Payment History		Strong	

Note: *There may be exceptions where individual guidelines may be exceeded as municipal credits should be reviewed in total.*

GENERAL GUIDELINES FOR EVALUATING
ESSENTIAL PURPOSE REVENUE BONDS
(Water, Sewer, Electricity, etc.)

Population	>	1,000	Local
	>	3,000	Regional
Debt Coverage *(Revenue covenants should be at least 1.10 times the debt requirements.)*	>	1.10x	
Overall Economic and Financial Condition		Stable	
Financial Statements and Trends		Steady	
Top 10 Taxpayers Taxable Property as a % of Assessed Valuation	<	25%	
Concentration of Users of Systems		Absent	
User Charges Compared To Peers		Comparable	
Useful Life of Project		Term of Bonds	
Debt Repayment History		Consistent	
Total Debt to Assessed	<	25%	

Note: *There may be exceptions where individual guidelines may be exceeded as municipal credits should be reviewed in total.*

The Terms Of Bonds Selected

The term, or maturity, of the bond you select is critical — it determines how long you will receive the tax-free income stream.

If you select long-term bonds for your nest egg when interest rates are low, you will most likely have a loss in market value on these bonds until they mature. This is a good example of not having an adequate margin of safety, as Ben Graham always suggested.

The Yield Curve Is Talking

One of the most powerful tools I use to help select the proper term of the taxable or tax-free bonds we buy is the shape, or slope, of the yield curve.

This is not a perfect science but the basics are that steep yield curves (most often seen during economic slowdowns) usually lead to flat yield curves (economic slowdown back to recovery), which often lead back to steep yield curves again. These events do not always occur in perfect sequence, unfortunately, or bond selection would be super easy.

Rarely, there is a very brief inverted yield curve (economic peak) that presents itself between the two steps above. Inverted yield curves have usually been excellent bond buying opportunities as they often lead to lower interest rates. You may wish to store this fact in memory.

YIELD CURVES: THE BASICS

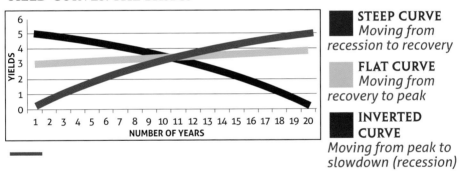

STEEP CURVE
Moving from recession to recovery

FLAT CURVE
Moving from recovery to peak

INVERTED CURVE
Moving from peak to slowdown (recession)

There also are historical averages that bond investors may use that illustrate when the shape of the yield curve is out of the ordinary, and these relationships can be helpful. In the stock market, a parallel comparison tool might be the Price to Earnings (PE) ratio, as both use historical relationships to help investors make more informed investment decisions.

For example, the widest 25-year average difference between short- and long-term interest rates (based on 91-day treasury bills and 30-year treasury bonds) is 460 basis points. At the time of this writing, the yield curve is ultra flat, as that spread is only 292 basis points. This makes sense market-wise as we are slowly digging out of the deep recession of 2008-2009, and the economy has improved, but is certainly not peaking.

Another Rule of Thumb for Bonds

Another crosscheck for calculating the shape and slope of the yield curve is to add 160 basis points (1.6%) to the current annualized consumer price index. Over the past 30 years, this has been a handy tool for determining what the historically correct long-term bond yields should be, given the current inflation rate. Like most relationships, it is not perfect.

The difference between the current yield on the bond you are studying and the inflation rate is called its term premium, and term premiums have definitely been shrinking. I think this is due mostly to global demand for dollar-denominated U.S. bonds and the effects of globalization. The world is a small place now, and inflation has generally been declining since 1979!

10-Year Treasury Yield Minus Inflation *	
Over The Past	**%**
5 years	1.03
10 years	1.33
20 years	2.38
30 years	3.40
40 years	2.65
50 years	2.54
*Inflation as measured by Non-Core CPI.	

Better Sleep?

For many investors, tax-free bonds are one of the most important asset classes for preserving their nest eggs. It is important to remain as diversified geographically and by types of issuers as possible and also to purchase only high-quality bonds. In this way, it is possible to have the best of both worlds, that is, competitive yields and great sleep.

Buying lower quality municipal bonds for a little extra yield is one of the most expensive mistakes investors make!

NEST EGG

THE ART OF REBALANCING YOUR NEST EGG

To keep on plan, check your percentage asset allocations at least once a year.

Maintenance Dose: Once Yearly

Hopefully you've settled on a system of organizing to keep the facts and figures of your nest egg updated and at your fingertips.

Now let's discuss the rebalancing you should do at least once a year. When markets are volatile and strategic opportunities present themselves, you may need to make adjustments more frequently.

At least annually, usually in December or early January, I take a hard look at how each asset class has performed for the year. An abundance of investment performance information is collected by the industry and made public at the end of each calendar year.

The Wall Street Journal and New York Times, for example, each do an excellent job of summarizing results in pull-out sections published in early January. I always look forward to those editions!

Our nest egg record system gives us the returns for each piece of our pie chart. This is a nice feature, which makes it easy to see how each slice of the pie has done for the year.

Then, I ask myself the following 10 questions:

1 How did the markets perform in general this year versus last year?

2 Which asset class did best?

3 Which asset class did worst?

4 Are there great American companies or industries that had something very unusual happen that is likely a one-time anomaly?

5 Did we have too many or too few individual asset classes?

6 How did large caps, mid caps, small caps and foreign stocks perform in relation to each other? (See definitions for these later in the chapter.)

7 Should we add to or subtract from any sectors to adjust our overall Beta and potential for Alpha given what has happened this year in the markets?

8 What would be the absolute most difficult contrarian (opposite of the herd) reallocation move to make now, given this year's performance results?

9 What, in theory, is the single biggest overall mistake we could make now? (A Howard Marks favorite question.)

10 And finally: How does our nest egg's market risk formula look today versus one year ago given what happened in the markets this year and the fact that we are one year older?

Things to Check Daily or Weekly

I am often asked if there are things I think nest egg builders should check more often. I have built a list of easy-to-find things that you may want to consider following either daily or weekly:

1 The Dow Jones Industrial Average (only 30 stocks).

2 The S&P 500 and Nasdaq stock indices.

3 The current yield on the benchmark U.S. 10-year Treasury note and the 30-year Treasury bond.

4 The general economic trend in terms of annualized GDP growth percentage.

5 The current U.S. unemployment rate.

6 Where we are in the presidential election cycle.

7 The slope (difference in yield between short-term and long-term bonds) of the U.S. Treasury yield curve.

All of these things can be found easily in most large daily newspaper business sections or on the Internet. I have a favorites page on my phone that quickly shows me where the markets and funds we own are trading each day. It was easy to set up.

There are lots of good options. You can build a "watch list" as simple or as complex as you wish. Remember, Ben Graham said we need to be "patient, disciplined and eager to learn."

If you would like to "kick it up a notch," as chef Emeril Lagasse is fond of saying about his culinary objectives, here are more crosschecks:

8 The current Price-to-Earnings (PE) multiple of the stock market vs. the historical PE average of 16.7 times earnings since 1982. This tells you if the market is cheap or expensive compared to historical averages.

9 The reciprocal of the current PE ratio with the current yield on the U.S. 10-year Treasury note. This will help you determine the advantage of stocks vs. bonds.

10 The current flow of funds into stocks vs. bonds (to reveal excessive pendulum swings and what the herd is doing with their excess cash).

11 The current strength or weakness of the Dollar vs. our main trading partner currencies like the Japanese Yen, the Chinese Yuan Renminbi and the Euro.

12 The amount of investor cash sitting on the sidelines (a fear gauge).

13 The current quarter and year-over-year real estate and new car sales trends (for a look at how consumers are feeling and spending).

14 What Warren Buffett and Howard Marks are currently thinking and recommending, as well as other experts like John Waggoner, formerly of USA Today, and Randall Forsyth of Barrons.

Friendly Suggestions for Avoiding Big Nest Egg Rebalancing Mistakes

It will be very, very tempting each year to add new cash to the best performing or "hot" asset classes from the previous year and avoid adding new cash to the under-performers. Although this one-sided "chase the hot sector" strategy works when prices in the hot categories are increasing, you must have the discipline to constantly review your mix percentages and adjust your percentages in each asset class. I like to make these adjustments in baby steps.

If you only chase winners each year, you are increasing the likelihood of a bad nest egg market experience down the road. History provides many examples. You also must be willing to cull losers, especially if they have not performed well during a period when everything else did. Think of the culling as if you were pulling weeds from your garden.

Dogs of the Dow Strategy

A strategy actually exists whereby investors try to buy the 10 worst performing (in terms of price) stocks in the 30-stock Dow Jones Industrial Average.

The underlying theory is that these huge, diverse companies, which have met strict qualifying requirements to be part of the Dow, at some

PEARLS OF WISDOM
How you allocate (and rebalance) your investments among the different asset classes often accounts for 90 percent or more of your nest egg's success.

point will turn around their profits and stock prices. This is a leap of faith in the capitalistic system, of course.

I believe Ben Graham and Warren Buffett would approve.

First, one must look up the current dividend yield for each Dow stock. You can find them on the Internet. The formula then is to divide the last 12 months' dividend payouts by the current price of each Dow stock. It is assumed that in order to be a dog in the first place the company's stock price must have fallen. This mathematically makes these companies' dividend yields the highest in the Dow average.

For example, because AT&T stock has fallen so much recently and its dividend is unchanged, the denominator of the function is much smaller in the formula. This makes the dividend yield (5.48 percent) the highest in the Dogs of the Dow list at the time of this writing.

You are, in theory, buying the cheapest of the very best, hopefully with a margin of safety. (For more information, you can visit www.dogsofthedow.com.)

As this is written, John Waggoner of USA Today has identified the Dow Dogs as:

AT&T (ticker T)	Pfizer (PFE)	Caterpillar (CAT)
Verizon (VZ)	General Electric (GE)	ExxonMobil (XOM)
Chevron (CVX)	Merck (MRK)	Coca-Cola (KO)
McDonalds (MCD)		

It will be fun to see how this countercyclical strategy plays out in the coming years!

Note: The Dogs of the Dow investment strategy is for informational purposes only to illustrate contrarian, or opposite thinking and should not be considered as investment advice or as a recommendation. The author is not registered to recommend stock/mutual fund strategies or individual transactions.

Know Your Asset Classes

It helps to have a basic understanding of the various asset classes available for your nest egg so you can be confident that you're truly accomplishing your rebalancing goals each year.

Morningstar, which provides research on investments of all kinds, does an excellent job of defining the various asset classes. The research firm started doing it in 1996 and currently follows 110 investment categories.

Morningstar defines three major domestic asset classes for stocks or stock mutual funds found in nest eggs today.

You'll need a definition of "market cap." A company's market capitalization is simply the number of common stock shares it has outstanding multiplied by its current stock price. (Within each general capitalization category, there usually are three subcategories: **Value, Blend** and **Growth**.)

Large Cap Stocks or Mutual Funds: These are the largest companies in the stock market – generally those with market caps of more than $8 billion, or whose capitalization falls in the top 70 percent of the U.S. stock market. These examples are household names:

Walmart	General Electric	Apple

Mid cap stocks or Mutual Funds: These are medium-sized companies with market capitalizations that fall between $1 billion and $8 billion. They usually represent 20 percent of the total market capitalization of the U.S. stock market. For example:

Williams-Sonoma	Dollar Thrift Automotive	Dun & Bradstreet

Small Cap Stocks or Mutual Funds: These are small companies with market capitalizations of less than $1 billion. They usually fall in the bottom 10 percent of total stock market capitalization. You've probably heard of these, too:

Red Lion Hotels	Jack in the Box	Monroe Muffler Brake

The most interesting and important thing about these three major market categories is that they all perform differently, depending on the stage of any economic cycle.

It makes sense that the largest companies are the most stable and generally produce steady dividend payment records and more stable overall stock prices – in other words, lower Betas.

Mid cap and small cap stocks tend to have higher growth rates and also tend to be less focused on dividends and more focused on growth, which can produce more price volatility. These are growing companies that tend to borrow more to fund their growth but may produce exceptional returns if the company succeeds.

I also like to own foreign stocks (in a smaller percentage than domestic stocks) of great global companies. They serve as both a hedge and a diversification tool to balance domestic stocks we own. Like bonds, foreign stocks can create a counterbalancing force to reduce our nest egg's overall Beta, or price sensitivity risk. When we zig, they usually zag.

Hitting Singles or Home Runs?

In a baseball context, I think of large caps as singles hitters with lots of base runners, mid caps as doubles and triples hitters and small caps as home run hitters and an occasional unexpected strike out. It makes sense to have some of each category in your nest egg.

I also like to use the Dogs of the Dow contrarian theory with these three market capitalization types, overweighting the out of favor class a little each year. I can hear Ben Graham reminding me that we can only manage risk, not returns, when I make these minor mix adjustments.

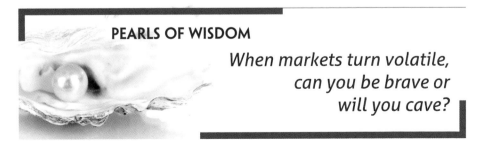

PEARLS OF WISDOM

*When markets turn volatile,
can you be brave or
will you cave?*

The Economic Cycle and Market Cap Performance

Over the past 30 years, each U.S. economic cycle has had an average life span of 4-4 1/2 years. The most recent cycle, however, has been much longer, perhaps because the market decline in 2008-2009 was the most dramatic since the Great Depression. Though it's hardly a perfect rule, you can generally assume that each market cap type will follow the economic cycle in the following way:

In very general terms, small cap stocks have historically performed better than large cap stocks but the tradeoff is that they often have much more price volatility. It is much easier for a successful small company to grow but this carries a greater risk that a particular small company might not.

What if their only product suddenly loses its patent protection or other competitors try to seize the same market niche? Larger cap companies are more likely to have a diverse product line and broader distribution channels to offset the unexpected.

In general, small cap stocks tend to lead us out of difficult economic periods or recessions, as they have the ability to more quickly turn up or turn down production of their products. As the economy matures and starts to peak, however, large cap stocks tend to perform better due to their diversification and established business plans.

Mid cap stocks have characteristics of both large and small caps. They tend to have lower Betas but, in theory, also produce less Alpha.

Our family model has been to own all three market capitalizations as well as strong foreign company stocks and use contrarian thinking to overweight the monthly investments in the worst-performing class.

This is a simple strategy, but it has worked well for us in our nest egg plan.

Will You Outlive Your Nest Egg?

I think almost everyone worries about this possibility. For one thing, Americans are living much longer than past generations. In general, this makes the nest egg investing program more important than it was for our parents.

Our general assumption is that we will use our nest egg for 30 years after we decide to retire.

Wall Street experts often suggest that you can draw 3-7 percent of your nest egg each year to live on (based on historical market returns minus inflation) and still not outlive it.

This rule of thumb ignores the fact that we may or may not receive or be eligible for Social Security in our later years. If we do receive Social Security, we see it as a bonus program.

Social Security certainly needs a makeover and it will probably mean extending the age qualification and perhaps add some means testing. In other words, you may have to show the government your nest egg to qualify for Social Security in the future. The following chart estimates the amount of money you could withdraw monthly, at three different percentages, based on the size of your nest egg.

THIRTY-YEAR MONTHLY RETIREMENT CALCULATOR

	MONTHLY WITHDRAWAL AMOUNT		
Nest Egg Size	@3%	@5%	@7%
$50,000.	$211	$268	$333
$100,000	$422	$537	$665
$250,000	$1054	$1342	$1663
$500,000	$2108	$2684	$3327
$1,000,000*	$4216	$5368	$6653
$3,000,000*	$12648	$16104	$19959
$5,000,000*	$21080	$26840	$33265
			extrapolated from $500k

Be Prepared!

The Social Security debate and solution may take decades! We now have about 320 million Americans and the retiring Baby Boomer class, the largest ever, is retiring at an 18,000-worker-per-day pace. I think the best advice for these unsolved issues is in the Boy Scout motto: Be Prepared!

NEST EGG

THINKING IN OPPOSITES

Think of it this way: When apples are expensive, buy oranges.

Keep Perspective Always

You can never assume that the investments you have selected for your nest egg will always produce positive returns.

There have been many periods in the 128-year history of the stock market when investors not only didn't make money, a single penny, but endured huge paper losses, or, if they sold out, real losses. Between 1997 and 2007, the stock market basically had no gain at all!

I think being regularly reminded of these turbulent periods and sudden market drops is an important part of keeping the stock market in perspective – which in many cases means controlling the urge to sell everything. As Warren Buffett learned very early in his investing career, it pays to be patient and hold on.

Market Bubbles Throughout History

Following are examples of a few classic market bubbles that eventually burst. For a better understanding of these periods, I am indebted to, among others, the research and writing of financial analyst and Forbes contributor Jesse Colombo.

Dutch Tulip Speculation (1634-1637)

The Ottoman Empire of what is now Turkey introduced the tulip to Europe in the 16th Century. An elegant new plant, its beauty quickly captured the fancy of the populace. The unique, intense color of the petals had an almost hypnotic effect on Europeans, especially in the Netherlands. In Dutch high society, tulip bulbs became a status symbol. Soon people were buying as many as possible, speculating that they could be sold later for great profit.

Tulip bulb speculation rose to such a pitch that some Dutch investors actually sold all of their land and other worldly possessions for a single bulb.

Prices soared to tens of thousands of dollars per bulb and many who owned them became extraordinarily wealthy. In the later stages of the bubble, no bulbs actually traded hands. Paper contracts were executed without the bulbs being present, hinting at the fragility of the tulip bulb market.

In 1637, tulip prices suddenly and unexpectedly collapsed, throwing the Netherlands into a mild economic depression.

Many have speculated that the collapse was triggered by an outbreak of the bubonic plague, which in 1636 killed 14 percent of the population of the Dutch city of Haarlem, the center of tulip speculation. Choosing life over livelihood, traders stayed away in droves. The sudden deflation in prices correlates with the historical model, which shows that speculative bubbles often end abruptly and painfully, which "tulipmania" certainly did.

PEARLS OF WISDOM

You must always be willing to invest at the moment of maximum pessimism.

The Stock Market Crash of 1929

The most dramatic stock market crash in American history occurred in 1929, at the end of a prosperous post-World War I economic period commonly referred to as the Roaring 20s. Using borrowed money in many instances, investors enthusiastically bought up the stocks of new commercial products like automobiles and airplanes. The buying frenzy drove the stock market to new highs.

By the fall of 1929, however, the stock market had peaked and a market crash like no other unfolded. It led directly to 1,200 bank failures, 25 percent unemployment and, eventually, the Great Depression. The stock market itself lost 90 percent of its value!

It may be almost impossible to imagine losing almost all of your stock portfolio in one single crash, but it happened.

Adding to the uncertainty of the era, President Franklin D. Roosevelt abruptly ended the gold standard in 1933 (before that, all U.S. currency had to be backed dollar-for-dollar in gold bullion) and also prohibited private ownership of gold except for jewelry. Former Fed Chairman Ben Bernanke, an expert on the Depression, called studying this turbulent period "the Holy Grail of Macroeconomics." He was certainly correct.

Japan's Commercial Real Estate Bubble of the 1980s

Japan has been fighting deflation forces for almost 30 years. Many economists trace the beginning of the problem to the wild speculation in commercial real estate in Tokyo between 1986 and 1991.

The U.S. and other allies had helped rebuild Japan after World War II. Led by the electronics and automobile industries, Japan over time became one of the strongest economies in the world. Commercial brands like Sony and Toyota are world leaders.

Beginning in 1986, there was wild speculation in Japanese real estate, especially in the Tokyo residential and commercial markets. That runaway market peaked in 1989, as the Japanese Nikkei market index rose to over 40000. Then the highly inflated stock and property markets began to crash and, by 1992, the Nikkei had plunged to 15000. This period in Japan's economic history is often referred to as the "Lost Decades," and the deflationary pressures from it still exist today.

Black Monday, October 19, 1987

The largest one-day crash in U.S. stock market history occurred on this day. The Dow Jones Industrial Average stood at 875 at the end of 1981 and then rose dramatically over the next several years to peak at over 2700 in August 1987.

It was a market run-up fueled by leveraged buyouts of companies and merger mania. As the market started to slide lower in early October, an avalanche of sell orders created a panic on Wall Street. On October 19, the Dow index toppled, losing a total of 508 points in one day for an incredible 22.6 percent loss.

The Dot-Com Collapse in the Late 1990s

The earliest Internet technology companies in the 1990s were often called "Dot-coms" because of the .com moniker attached to each company's web site. Their main product was software for

the new personal computer that was changing the way Americans (and soon the world) did everything. Companies on the ground floor of the revolution prospered exponentially.

The problem was that guessing which dot-com would hit it big became a speculator's sport and the NASDAQ stock index, which was heavily over-weighted with technology companies at the time, rose to over 5000 before crashing.

At the time of this writing, we have surpassed 5000 again, so this has everyone's attention. Only about 43 percent of the NASDAQ is now made up of technology companies, so the index is much more diversified and theoretically less subject to market crashes over a single type of business or innovation.

Barings Bank Collapse in 1995

Barings Bank in England was founded in 1762, financed the Napoleonic Wars and was the personal bank of Queen Elizabeth. But in 1995, a rogue trader by the name of Nick Leeson forced the 233-year old institution into bankruptcy.

Leeson's job at Barings was trading what were supposed to be low-risk derivative contracts to create arbitrage between the Singapore Mercantile Exchange and Japan's Osaka Exchange. He conducted unauthorized trades, which eventually cost Barings $1.4 billion and brought on its eventual demise.

Remember, the only perfect hedge is a shrub.

U.S. Real Estate Speculation Anyone?

The main culprit in what we now call the Great Recession of 2008-2009 was poorly underwritten home mortgages. You could feel the greed pendulum swinging as people chased what seemed like an easy, painless entry into homeownership.

Other speculators set about buying several homes with mortgage payments that were reduced or deferred, until the homes could be "flipped" in a seemingly ever-increasing housing price environment. Toss in the fact that many of the mortgages were essentially rated as riskless by several professional rating agencies, packaged into securities and then sold to unwitting investors and you have a formula for disaster.

When the bubble burst, the sudden collapse in real estate values nearly pushed the U.S. economy into another Great Depression.

Under the contrarian-investing hypothesis, however, it was a perfect time to buy a larger new or second home, or a condo in Colorado. Interest rates were very low due to the crisis and there were many more sellers than buyers. It's an example of the value of "opposite thinking" and having the extra cash on hand to invest during extremely volatile and severe market drops.

Of Course, Owning No Stocks is OK!

Reading about these horrific crashes and single-day drops in the market may be testing your appetite for owning common stocks or stock-based mutual funds. As I mentioned earlier, there are many very wealthy investors who own no stocks because of the potential roller coaster of the stock market and the anxiety it causes when they see red ink in their stock portfolio.

PEARLS OF WISDOM

No mistakes, no experience.
No experience, no wisdom.

The greatest fear for many investors is that they might need access to their money precisely as the stock market is in a sharp correction. That is why Ben Graham said you should always have at least 25 percent in liquid reserves.

The most important thing about nest egg design is that it perfectly fits your very personal risk tolerance. If you simply cannot tolerate market volatility, a portfolio of evenly laddered bonds and bank CDs with compounding interest is just right for you. Remember that while stocks clearly have been shown to be capable of creating great wealth, bonds are better tools to help keep your hard-earned wealth intact.

The Stock Market is On a Roll

At the time of this writing, all three major stock market indices (Dow, S&P 500 and the NASDAQ) are at or near all-time highs, so it's easy to be optimistic and perhaps even euphoric. It is also easy to become complacent since basically all asset classes are going up in price and it appears that this trend will continue for some time.

This makes it one of the best times to start thinking about the possibility of totally opposite market conditions! If you need to make changes in your asset allocation mix, the best time to do this is when prices are increasing, as you will book gains rather than losses.

PEARLS OF WISDOM

Compound interest is the eighth wonder of the world. He who understands it, earns it ... he who doesn't ... pays it.

- Albert Einstein

Remember the Four Most Important Things

We discussed in the introduction to this book the four things that, I think, lead most often to long-term nest-egg building success:

1. **When you start.** As early as possible.

2. **How much you invest each month.** As much as you can afford and still enjoy life.

3. **The mix of investments you select.** You now know more about managing risk, how to allocate assets and learn from historical returns — and that even a 50-50 stock-to-bond ratio does pretty well over the years.

4. **How you react when markets turn volatile and sharply downward.** You have to take the long-term view, not panic, and be patient.

Finally, let's think about number 4 since the opposite market conditions – all-time highs in stock prices – exist now.

Oil Prices Crash, Interest Rates Stay Low

There have been two huge surprises in the markets at the time of this writing. First, virtually no one thought interest rates would continue to fall after the Federal Reserve stopped dominating the U.S. bond market last year with its historic bond buying, or quantitative easing program. It was counterintuitive that interest rates would fall even further as the economy finally stabilized. Virtually every market expert on Wall Street had interest rates normalizing to higher levels last year.

Second, and perhaps more shocking, was that experts did not foresee the price of oil falling almost 50 percent! As the consumer has now clearly benefitted both financially and psychologically from cheaper gasoline, everyone is wondering if this drop is temporary or more lasting.

Using the "thinking in opposites" philosophy, I am wondering, and doing research on, which oil and oil service companies now might make good long-run investments. I noticed that Exxon, the world's fourth largest oil company, is now one of the Dogs of the Dow!

Which companies have dropped so much in price that Buffet's "margin of safety" might possibly exist now? What would Howard Marks think about the downside limits in these investments? These are great examples of applying opposite or contrarian thinking to the current market.

In our hypothetical scenario, are the falling prices of the stocks of great American companies a long-term opportunity and not something that you should panic over?

Rechecking the Risk Formula

With the stock market roaring, I'm also recalculating our family nest egg risk formula (discussed in Chapter 5) to determine if we should shift some cash from stocks to safer choices like cash or bonds.

This is a difficult move to consider now, which makes me think it is probably the right thing to do, again using the "think opposites" philosophy.

The temptation is to shift even more cash into stocks now that they are steadily rising and the economy is performing much better, but I know what Ben Graham would say: Chasing returns is one of the most expensive things investors can do!

PEARLS OF WISDOM

Beware of the TINA trade...investing in something new or trendy because There Is No Alternative. Hold cash instead.

Remember, it is always your choice to underweight or overweight the risk formula. Only you know your tolerance for market volatility.

Waiting for the Home Run

Sometimes there are opportunities to use opposite thinking even in non-financial endeavors.

The Kansas City Royals baseball team had its greatest success during the George Brett years, 1973-1993. KC's only Hall of Famer, Brett is usually placed in the top tier of elite hitters of all time. In addition, he was totally loyal to the Royals organization, is a great dad, and gives a lot of his time to charities, qualities I admire greatly.

The Royals won the pennant in 1980 and were World Series champs in 1985. This was a remarkable feat for a small market Major League baseball team, and a tribute to the dreams and commitment of owner Ewing Kauffman, who underwrote many losing seasons.

During the rebuilding years, our family remained loyal supporters and kept methodically upgrading our seat selections. We were, in effect, investing a little more each year in the "stock" of the KC Royals. We gradually moved to seats on the aisle, out of the rain and sun, and closer and closer to the coveted foul ball zone and the Dippin' Dots ice cream stand, which my boys supported with great enthusiasm.

Fast forward to 2014 and the Royals shocked the baseball world with their incredible run through the playoffs to win the American League pennant, their first since 1985!

Because we had been loyal season ticket holders and fans (and opposite thinkers while the Royals were losing), we were rewarded with seats to purchase for each of the Playoff and World Series games. The already valuable tickets became hotter with every game the Royals played on their march to the World Series championship game.

We could easily have tripled our money by selling our tickets but there was no way we would miss this incredible opportunity to see the boys in blue perform so well. I was so glad we had used the opposites theory years before this historic season.

Buy Your Snow Blower This Summer?

Opposite thinking can apply to everyday events and hopefully increase your chances for creating Alpha everywhere. Whether it's waiting for the Thursday two-for-one burger day to go out to eat, or buying a snow blower in the middle of summer, opposite thinking is a lifetime project for helping your nest egg grow faster and larger, while having more fun too.

A simple way to directly apply opposite or contrarian thinking is to follow the positive and negative changes in market values in each of the asset classes in your nest egg. Now that you hopefully have a nest egg building system in place either on paper or in electronic form, this really is a pretty simple process.

What you are looking for each month are the categories in your nest egg pie chart that are rising or falling in value. Each month, you should be adding as much cash as you can afford to your nest egg and it is very tempting to simply add all your cash to the asset classes that are going up. It feels like the right thing to do and is easy to accomplish.

A very good cross check for practicing contrarian rather than herd investing is that each time you invest, your emotions will be pushing you very hard to do the exact opposite of what you know you really should do. This can often produce what I call "queasy stomach time." But it can lead to great things, like creating Alpha on the way to increasing your net worth.

While it is certainly a good idea to add regularly to each class you have selected, contrarian investing suggests that you slightly overweight the asset classes that are falling and underweight the ones that are going up.

If you think about it, this process is just dollar cost averaging, like the bond ladder process we discussed in Chapter 6. You are effectively lowering your cost basis in each asset class that you are slightly overweighting with each monthly investment, and the losses should eventually turn into gains if you are patient and consistent.

If you perform this simple, mechanical ritual with each month's nest egg addition, you are greatly increasing the chances for having a successful nest egg when you retire. On your brokerage statement, just look for the red numbers, or losses, in individual asset classes. If you are a more aggressive investor, you may wish to direct all of your monthly nest egg investment to the asset class with the largest paper loss to lower your overall cost basis.

Stocks do not always increase in value. Over long periods of time, focusing on buying low and selling high – contrarian strategy – has served many investors (stock and bond investors, real estate owners and even sports fans) very well.

Now, in Chapter 9, let's explore the parts of the brain that directly control our emotions as we build a nest egg.

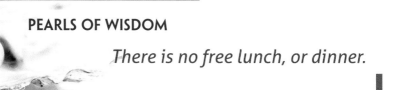

PEARLS OF WISDOM

There is no free lunch, or dinner.

NEST EGG

DAYDREAMING PAYS: INVESTING AND YOUR BRAIN

The author encourages daydreaming.
Take a little time every day to disconnect.

What's In There?

I have always been fascinated with the human brain. The more I learn about this immensely powerful organ only the size of a grapefruit, weighing at most three pounds and yet containing billions of complex electrical circuits, the more I am simply astounded.

With over one hundred billion neuron connections, one's brain acts like a supercomputer for our body as it controls our thinking, pulse rate, blood pressure and many other activities . Besides performing critical body functions, parts of your brain can be directly tied to investing emotions like fear and greed, and we will explore these specific aspects further in this chapter.

Here's your brain, and a short list of structures and what they do.

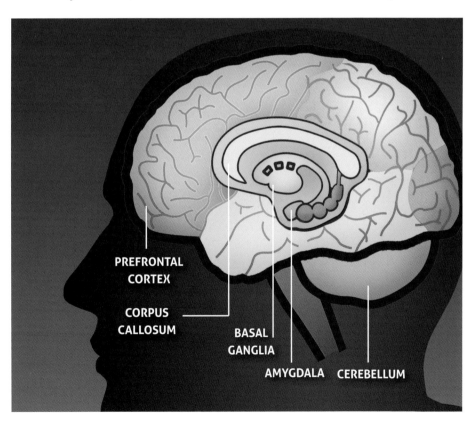

1 **Prefrontal Cortex:** located directly behind your forehead, this is the part of the brain that controls your thoughts and how you respond to outside stimuli. It is the last part of the brain to develop and is sometimes referred to as the center for sober thought.

2 **Cerebellum:** physical coordination is centered here as well as higher learning like mathematics and music. Social skills may be developed here.

3 **Corpus Callosum:** this bundle of nerves connects the right and left sides of the brain. This part of the brain is often associated with creativity as well as problem solving.

4 **Amygdala:** this is the emotional center of the brain where fear and greed are thought to be managed. For adults, emotions are also filtered by the prefrontal cortex.

5 **Basal Ganglia:** this part of the brain acts as the manager of information for the prefrontal cortex. Small and large motor movements are believed to be controlled here also.

It is thought that development of the brain starts at the back and moves toward the front as one ages, and this helps explain many events from our boys' teenage and college years much better. There are four lobes to the brain as well: the occipital, parietal, temporal and frontal.

My Brother John, the Scientist

One of the reasons for my interest was that my oldest brother, John, was a pioneer in the field of researching the map of the brain. He provided physics support for the development of Positron Emission Tomography (PET Scan) while he worked at Johns Hopkins University. He later founded the Neurological Visualization Laboratory at the University of Virginia in Charlottesville and then became the Medical Imaging Program Manager for the workstation division of the Hewlett Packard Computer Company based in Boston. Later, he was President and cofounder of Sectra, North America, a medical systems company based in Sweden.

His main focus was designing a computer program that connected thousands of brain scans into one picture so that one's brain could be quickly studied and evaluated without the need for exploratory surgery, which can often carry a lot of risks.

He contributed to an article for National Geographic magazine and also presented his work at the Smithsonian Institution in Washington. He owned six patents in the medical imaging field and authored over 20 scientific publications. Even though he was my older brother and he pounded me a lot , it is probably safe to say he was brilliant.

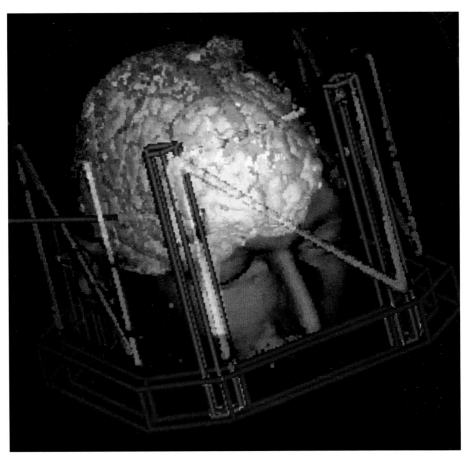

John's brain as pictured in a June 1995 National Geographic special section, "Quiet Miracles of the Brain."

After attending the U.S. Naval Academy and then earning his Masters degree at Penn State, John went on to complete another Masters degree and his Ph.D. in Computer Programming at Rensselaer Polytechnic Institute (RPI) in Albany, New York.

I remember John visiting my Mom and me at our home in Kansas during a summer break. He had brought the head of a Barbie doll (Ken, to be more precise) with him. Throughout the weekend, he kept rotating the doll head in his hand in many directions, as if he was mentally photographing all the possible angles one might view using multiple Cat (CT) scans.

We thought this Barbie doll activity was very strange...yet somehow very normal for John. This was a guy who often read books in the dugout during Little League baseball games to maximize his learning opportunities while awaiting his turn to bat. Why would anyone just sit there and waste time waiting to bat?

Movie Special Effects

One of the legendary John stories in our small town occurred after John the scientist released about 200 lightning bugs one summer evening in our local movie theatre to create what John called the earliest "special effects" on the big screen. He had sneaked the jar of fireflies into the theatre at the bottom of an overflowing bag of popcorn. I think he was 12.

Management somehow connected him to the crime and after recapturing all the lightning bugs, John was promptly banned from seeing movies for the rest of the summer. I can still remember seeing his snapshot pasted in the front ticket box office: "Don't let this kid in!"

He was the state DeMolay champ with a .22 caliber rifle and he actually built a small rifle range in our basement, although there was not really room for one. He was fascinated by how bullets would change shape as they passed through different types of wooden blocks. On many summer days, my Mom would ask me what that pop was she had just heard coming from the basement. I told her it was probably just John dropping something. I am pretty sure she never really bought that story, but understood science was being conducted downstairs.

Little did we know that summer that John was using the Ken Barbie doll study to develop a way to computer image the brain in a three-dimensional view. This breakthrough would eventually greatly contribute to the development of the brain scan, which has undoubtedly helped save thousands of lives to date due to the elimination of dangerous exploratory brain surgery.

I would like to dedicate this chapter to my brother John, an avid pilot, as we tragically lost him in a military helicopter accident in Southern California in 2008, of which he was a passenger. It is safe to say he made a difference with his contributions to the medical field.

Where Investment Decisions Are Made

You have no doubt heard of Warren Buffet's quintessential, yet so simple advice for dealing with market emotions: "Be greedy when others are fearful and fearful when others are greedy." This is the essence of the counter cyclical investment, or thinking in opposites philosophy we have discussed in previous chapters. As I discussed in Chapter 8, you have to be willing to do things with your investments that seem like the opposite thing to do at that precise moment, and this always takes a great deal of discipline.

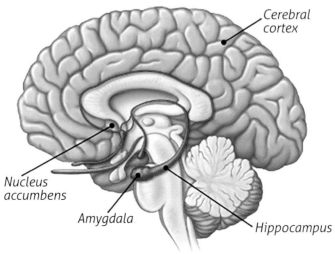

Cerebral cortex

Nucleus accumbens

Amygdala

Hippocampus

My research showed that there are basically two very specific parts of the brain that help us make either really good or really bad investment decisions because they relate directly to the forceful emotions of greed and fear.

I learned that greed is generally attributed to the Nucleus Accumbens, located in the prefrontal cortex. Because this area is the part of the brain most affected by alcohol and caffeine, it is often referred to as "the fun zone." You see it in high gear on college campuses on weekends.

I hear that a very popular party drink on college campuses now is to empty one half of a Red Bull caffeine "study aide" and then fill back the half-empty can with vodka. This, I am told, can fully stimulate the "fun zone," and I now understand why.

In investing, greed often tempts us as investors to follow the herd and make quick decisions when markets are volatile, often in the wrong direction. Greed also makes us chase higher returns and "new" investment strategies without really understanding completely why the returns are seemingly better than average.

Fear, on the other hand, is generally associated with the parietal lobe of the Anterior Insula, located at the back of your brain. Fear often encourages investors to sell when markets are falling and think on a very short term basis.

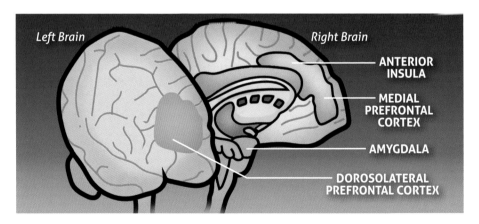

I find it fascinating that these two very specific emotions can be mapped so precisely to parts of our brain, and studies using electroencephalograms have confirmed the locations.

The "Aha" or "Eureka" Moment

Robert Lee Holtz of the Wall Street Journal published his collective research several years ago, and of particular interest to me was the explanation of why we often have those light bulb or moments of insight while relaxing, performing mechanical work like mowing grass, or driving or even when taking a shower.

I often find that my best and most creative ideas occur, for example, when I am jogging or mowing the grass. My brain is more active then.

Holtz's research showed that our brains are actually on higher alert with more electrical connections working together in a highly focused manner when we are daydreaming and our minds wander. He cited research by a team of doctors at Northwestern University in Chicago that identified a sudden burst of gamma rays in the brain's right hemisphere one third of a second (a very long period of time for the brain) before the " Eureka " moment hits us and a problem is solved or a name of a person is recalled. There must also be a rule that as we get older, we must have fewer and fewer of these moments of insightful clarity .

I often have more time to think strategically about my life, our nest egg and what the markets are doing when I am away from work or on a trip or vacation. It is really easy to miss the forest for the trees sometimes and I think it is a very healthy thing to daydream as much as humanly possible!

If you simplify the Nest Egg building process down, it seems to me that knowing when greed and fear are often present can help investors at least recognize when those forces are most likely to be present. One can then attempt to do the opposite of what these emotions are suggesting and therefore hopefully make better long-term decisions.

PEARLS OF WISDOM

If someone offers you something for free, you might not want to take too much.

FEAR AND GREED CHECKLIST

You are being too greedy when:	You are being too fearful when:
(overactive nucleus accumbens)	*(overactive anterior insula)*
1 You only buy past winners.	**1** You sell everything and go to cash.
2 You are willing to try something new or trendy	**2** You cannot seem to make a decision about investing.
3 You add new types of asset classes, even though you do not fully understand them.	**3** You do not own any growth investments at all.
4 You quickly invest larger than normal amounts of excess, low yielding, cash.	**4** Your stomach turns queasy and you freeze.

In conclusion, in the previous nine chapters, we have now completed what I would call the nuts and bolts of how to build your nest egg. Now let's switch gears and see how two wonderfully generous people have turned their nest eggs into something extraordinary.

NEST EGG

PROFILE IN GENEROSITY: CHRISTINE E. LYNN

Generosity frees the heart.

Givers From The Start

One of the greatest privileges during my career at UMB has been observing the generosity of Christine Lynn. Her family has a storied history of philanthropy in Kansas City and Boca Raton, Florida. She also is a great friend and supporter of our bank.

Christine's late husband, Eugene, was a member of UMB's Board of Directors for many years while leading Kansas City-based Universal Underwriters, a nationwide insurer of automobile dealerships.

Gene Lynn's office was on the eighth floor of the famous R.A. Long building at 10th Street and Grand Avenue, later the headquarters of the Federal Reserve Bank of Kansas City and now home to UMB Bank. Built in 1911, it was Kansas City's first high-rise steel-skeleton structure — a majestic, stylish building now listed on the National Historic Site registry.

On the first floor, in the 1950s, was the first drive-in "patio bank" in America, created by City National Bank, as we were known at the time. You can see a picture of the patio bank on the next page. Bank customers found it convenient to transact business without having to come inside the bank. It is still there today.

The R.A. Long Building at 10th and Grand.

An article in the Kansas City Business Journal by Rob Roberts on April 12, 2014, profiled the Lynn family's generosity in Kansas City.

Gene's uncle, James, was one of the city's greatest philanthropists from the 1920s through the early 1950s.

The nation's first drive-in patio bank at City National Bank, now UMB Bank.

One of the first drive-through banks in America, near 18th and McGee.

Born in 1892, James Lynn grew up on a farm outside Archibald, Louisiana, and left home and school when he was 14. Soon after, he began working for several different railroad station agents. In 1909, James became an accountant for the Missouri Pacific Railroad and was quickly promoted from assistant auditor to auditor, after which he left the railroad to complete his formal education.

He was admitted to the Missouri Bar at age 21 and became a Certified Public Accountant (CPA). As a young CPA, one of James' first clients was U.S. Epperson Underwriting Co. The firm's principal business was underwriting insurance for the Kansas City lumber baron, R.A. Long.

Long, the driving force behind construction of Kansas City's Liberty Memorial and the namesake for Longview, Washington, and Longview, Louisiana, owned 61 lumberyards, located mostly in Arkansas, Oklahoma and Louisiana.

James was named general manager of U.S. Epperson in 1917. One year later, he founded Universal Underwriters.

The Lynns gave Epperson House to the University of Missouri - Kansas City.

In the early 1950s, he and his wife, Freda Lynn, sold a portion of the park-like property on which their home was built near 63rd Street and Meyer Boulevard. The largest estate in Kansas City at the time, it included a 9-hole golf course. They agreed to sell the land well below its market value so that Research Medical Center could be built there. Today, Research is a 511-bed hospital serving Kansas City and the Midwest.

When Swope Park, home of the Kansas City Zoo, was expanding, the Lynns donated 15 acres of prime real estate to the cause. They gave the Epperson House, a 58-room Tudor-Gothic mansion, to the University of Missouri-Kansas City.

Moving The Business To Boca

In the 1950s, James Lynn turned over his business interests to his nephew, Gene Lynn, and in the mid-1960s Gene moved his insurance business from Kansas City to Boca Raton, Florida. It is safe to say that Boca benefitted greatly by Gene's decision to continue his commitment to philanthropy in Florida.

Gene and Christine Lynn have touched many lives in Boca Raton. The three principal beneficiaries of their generosity have been Florida Atlantic University, the Community College of Boca Raton (renamed Lynn University in 1991), and Boca Raton Regional Hospital.

They made a very large gift to Florida Atlantic University from their Lynn Foundation. The School of Nursing today is named after Christine, who is a registered nurse. She greatly enjoys seeing young nurses develop their skills. Gene endowed an eminent scholar chair in the School of Business.

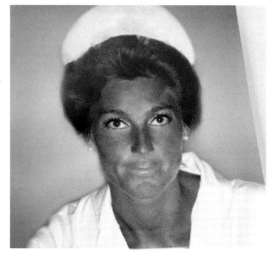

Christine on the day she graduated from nursing school.

Lynn University

Located three miles from the beach, Lynn University is a private university known for its international focus. It's consistently rated as one of the top international universities in America. Founded in 1962, it attracts students from the U.S. and 80 other nations. About one in four students is international.

The university attracted international attention in the 2012 presidential election when it hosted the final debate between President Barack Obama and former Massachusetts Gov. Mitt Romney.

It is also known for its online curricula, and was cited by U.S. News and World Report this year as having one of the nation's best online bachelor degree programs.

The Passing Of Gene Lynn

Gene Lynn died November 29, 1999, from complications following back surgery. His long-time friend Don Ross, president of Lynn University, stated afterward that Gene "was a gentle human being who did not like fanfare or a fuss made over him. He always felt it was better to give than receive."

The residence center, the library and the international school of communications were all named in honor of the Lynns and their generosity.

"Christine's unwavering generosity and her profound commitment to the university is unsurpassed. She and Gene have always risen to the occasion," Ross said.

Christine Lynn continued her generosity after her husband's death. She currently is chairman of the board of directors of Boca Raton Regional Hospital.

Like many generous people, the Lynns grew interested in the needs of many institutions and made contributions that profoundly changed what those facilities could offer. Boca Raton Regional Hospital is one example.

The Christine Lynn Heart And Vascular Institute

The Christine Lynn Heart and Vascular Institute opened at Boca Raton Regional Hospital in 2006. Since then, the institution has been named one of America's Best 100 Hospitals for cardiac and stroke care and the number one program in Florida for cardiac surgery by Healthgrades, a company that ranks U.S. physicians, hospitals and health care providers.

The Institute is home to the first hybrid operating room in Palm Beach County, which means that it can do imaging in the sterile environment of the OR for multiple "open" procedures, including cardiac and vascular.

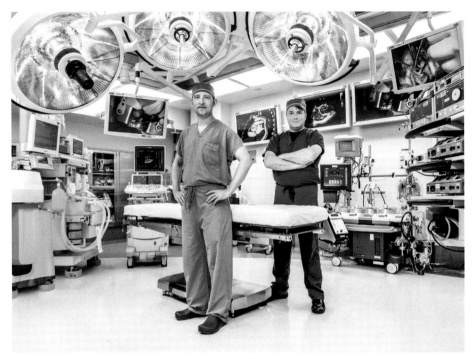

In the hybrid surgery suite at the Heart and Vascular Institute doctors can do imaging as they perform surgery. There's no moving of patients or time delays.

The Lynn Cancer Institute

Thanks to Christine's support, the Lynn Cancer Institute is a patient-centered, model facility that's widely considered the leading comprehensive cancer center in the area. It offers advanced radiation oncology, a medical infusion center, coordinated patient care through clinics specific to different cancers, clinical research and support groups.

In addition to standard radiation therapy for destroying tumors, Lynn patients have access to particle accelerators, which more precisely target the tumor, sparing healthy tissue. The center has five of the expensive machines, allowing it to treat approximately 1,100 patients annually with malignancies including breast, prostate, lung, brain and spinal tumors.

The more focused radiation often reduces the number of radiation treatments required. For example, a patient who normally would require 25-35 treatments may need only one to five using the accelerator.

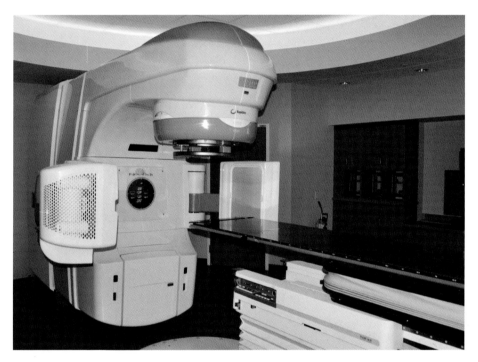

This Varian Novalis TX particle accelerator was installed when the Lynn Cancer Institute was built in 2005.

The Christine Lynn Women's Health and Wellness Institute

The latest addition to the hospital campus will be the Christine Lynn Women's Health and Wellness Institute. The 45,000-square foot building, for which ground was broken in April 2014, is funded by a $10 million gift from Christine and an additional $11 million in pledges.

Christine sees it as her chance to advance the level of care for women by providing centralized, integrated services in a warm and welcoming state-of-the-art environment.

As she often says, "I want to see great things happening while I am still around to see them."

The institute will offer a new breast cancer screening system approved last year by the FDA. The screening combines nine images taken of the breast at different angles into a 3-D view. It uses half the radiation of a

The 45,000 square foot building helps women by providing integrated, specialized services.

traditional mammogram and improves the radiologist's ability to differentiate cells that may by cancerous from those that are likely benign.

According to the company, the technology has reduced the number of required screening retakes by 40 percent, dramatically reducing patients' stress. To reduce anxiety during the test, an interactive experience distracts the patient by simultaneously stimulating the patient's sense of sight, smell and hearing.

Christine Lynn, a registered nurse, has continued through philanthropy to impact the world of health care.

In the Lynn Cancer Center lobby, the Wall of Hope is a changing tableau of 6 x 6-inch ceramic tiles, each with a message about a relationship with cancer. Every year, hospital patients, their families, hospital staff and physicians are invited to express themselves by decorating a tile. Patients often use their tile as a badge of survivorship and a record of their cancer-curing journey.

NEST EGG

PROFILE IN GENEROSITY: R. CROSBY KEMPER, JR.

A benefactor for our time.

One Man's Legacy

Another generous person with whom I've worked during my career at UMB is R. Crosby Kemper, Jr., former chairman of UMB Financial Corporation.

Crosby passed away on Jan. 2, 2014, at the age of 86. His legacy for Kansas City includes writing a blank check to save the Kansas City Symphony, building Kemper Arena to host the nationally acclaimed American Royal Livestock Show, and landing the Republican National Convention in 1976.

R. Crosby Kemper, Jr.

Birth of a Symphony

The Kansas City Philharmonic had been one of the main legs of the region's arts scene since 1896. In the early 1980s, it was unable to continue its mission and was about to close its doors. In 1982, as the season was about to be cancelled, Crosby provided the much-needed funding to recapitalize the orchestra. He would personally pay its losses. Today the Kansas City Symphony is one of the region's leading orchestras, with more than 50 concerts a year.

Over 80 full-time musicians perform for the symphony in the beautiful Kauffman Center for the Performing Arts. Built as part of Kansas City's downtown rejuvenation, the Kauffman Center was designed by the renowned architect Moshe Safdie and named in honor of Ewing and Irene Kauffman by their daughter, Julia. The symphony orchestra, led by celebrated conductor Michael Stern, also performs with the Lyric Opera and the Kansas City Ballet.

The Kansas City Symphony takes advantage of the superb acoustics and visual drama of the Kauffman Center's 1,600-seat Helzberg Hall.

Kemper, The American Royal, and Kansas City

The 116-year-old American Royal Livestock Show and Rodeo is held in the fall at Kemper Arena, the hall that Crosby built to honor his father, R. Crosby Kemper Sr. It's commonly described as the gem of Midwestern agricultural events.

The show's original purpose — to provide education and competitive learning experiences that promote hard work, leadership skills and agrarian values — hasn't changed since it opened in 1899 in the Kansas City Stockyards as the National Hereford Show. The horse show debuted in 1905.

Today, there are livestock exhibitions, a professional rodeo and one of the largest barbecue contests anywhere. It draws 270,000 and generates

Built in 18 months in 1973-'74 on the site of the former Kansas City Stock-yards, Kemper Arena was revolutionary in its simplicity and lack of interior columns obstructing views.

about $60 million in spending for Kansas City.

In 1969, the Royal was the reason for Kansas City's major league baseball team being named the Royals. (Crosby, by the way, was a part of the local ownership group formed to make sure the Kansas City Royals did not leave the city after its generous owner, Ewing Kauffman, passed away.)

The Beginning Of The AFA

Crosby also supported farm families and the agricultural way of life in other ways. He funded the Agricultural Future of America (AFA) to support agriculture and education when the blue-coated Future Farmers of America (FFA) abruptly moved its headquarters from Kansas City to Kentucky.

The FFA had been founded in 1928 by a group of farm boys at Kansas City's Baltimore Hotel. Crosby was determined to keep the tradition alive. The AFA provides scholarships and other educational opportunities supporting agriculture.

In 1985, when a large convention hotel was needed to revive downtown Kansas City, Crosby wrote a check and then made calls and wrote letters to raise the additional money needed, reportedly $35 million. Today, the hotel is part of the flagship Marriott Downtown, which includes the historic Muehlebach Hotel, where Harry S Truman learned he had beaten New York Gov. Thomas Dewey for the presidency, even though the then Chicago Daily Tribune reported the opposite.

A Better Place To Live

Crosby Kemper was fervently in favor of supporting the arts and making Kansas City a better place to live, conduct business and raise a family. He was outspoken on the subject and unafraid to stand up for things he believed furthered that goal. And at 6-feet-7-inches, he stood out, literally.

In 1990, he gave $6 million to build the Kemper Museum of Contemporary Art, located near Kansas City's Country Club Plaza, where everyone can view a changing collection of first tier modern art with no admission charge.

The Kemper Museum of Contemporary Art opened in 1994 featuring a central atrium. The prized bronze spider near the front entrance is by French-American artist and sculptor Louise Bourgeois.

"Portuguese Mother and Child," painted by William Paxton in the 1920s, illustrates Crosby Kemper's admonition to "buy what you like." It's now in the collection of UMB Bank.

It has certainly helped my education. From Crosby and the museum I learned about the art of Fairfield Porter, Jamie and Andrew Wyeth and Maxfield and Stephen Parrish, among many others.

For a man with the means to buy almost any art he wanted, Crosby always believed that the art you really enjoy is the art you should purchase, regardless of the artist, price or someone else's opinion.

One special Crosby story isn't about Kansas City.

One day Crosby heard that fast food restaurants were going to be built along the beautiful road leading to Monticello, Thomas Jefferson's ancestral home and gardens in Charlottesville, Virginia. I happened to be in his office at the time and it was clear that Crosby was not going to let that happen.

Jefferson was a scientist as well a statesman and he conducted many of his agricultural studies and experiments in the gardens there.

Crosby was a patriot and not about to let Monticello, a national treasure, be sullied. He contributed to purchase the land that today is referred to as Kemper Park.

There are many more stories of Crosby's anonymous giving and generosity, especially for UMB employee families in need and for civic support on local, regional and national stages. I simply don't have the room to list them all.

A fall view of the trail in Kemper Park on the road to Monticello.

The Soup Spoon Incident

I was lucky, to say the least, to get a job interview with R. Crosby Kemper and some top bank officers in the spring of 1981. The event occurred over lunch in Kansas City.

As I was midway to getting a spoonful of soup to my mouth, one of the senior bankers asked me yet another question. I nervously rested my soup spoon in the bowl as I collected my thoughts.

Crosby leaned over, and in his distinctive, deep voice said, "Jeff, you seem like a fine young man and I don't want to embarrass you. But I thought you might want to know you should never leave your soup spoon in the bowl. It always belongs at the side."

He said this in a very gracious manner, I'm sure only intending to give me a leg up in the business world, which I was fervently hoping to enter. I was completing my MBA from the University of Kansas in nearby Lawrence. I could feel my face flushing and my first thought was that I had blown the interview.

Crosby and I laughed about that lunch and the "soup spoon incident" many times over the years. My three sons and I have a standing rule now about where soup spoons should rest, and I now notice where other people place their soup spoons.

The many hours Crosby and I spent together over three decades discussing the markets, the economy, politics and interest rates is something I won't forget. It was the best real-world education about judging people, risk, banking and art that one could get. I will be forever grateful.

Crosby often said, with a twinkle in his eye, that he really enjoyed our discussions as the years passed — mostly because I seemed to agree with his opinion more and more.

It's clear to me from his generous gifts to Kansas City, that R. Crosby Kemper, Jr., left a remarkable legacy. I doubt that the city will ever see anyone as generous to the arts, music and the rich agricultural tradition of the region.

He will be missed.

The pond in Kemper Park.

NEST EGG

WHEN MUCH IS GRANTED, MUCH IS EXPECTED

If you can count it, it does not count.

It's the Fun Part

We finally arrive at what I hope will be the most fun and gratifying chapter of this book: How to turn a part of your hard-earned nest egg into something that can really make a difference.

First, let's define what making a difference means, as it obviously can mean very different things, all worthy, with different price tags.

Gardener-Principal-Philanthropist

My Dad was an elementary school principal for virtually his entire teaching career, and I learned a lot about generosity, kindness and making a difference from him.

When school was out each summer, Dad would always build a huge vegetable garden and then "enlist" my two older brothers and me to be the gardening staff. If we removed weeds, corn worms and potato bugs with the proper technique and in significant quantities in the morning, we could, after an inspection of our work, go swimming and play baseball in the afternoons and evenings. It seemed like a fair deal to us.

Dad used his job as principal of Lincoln School in Pittsburg, Kansas, and his summer garden as his means to make a difference and, in retrospect, I realize how lucky I was to be there to watch. While he practiced the "compassionate dictator" style of management at Lincoln School, he truly loved working with elementary students, their parents, and the teaching staff, all of whom were women. (That was very common in the 1950s and '60s.)

As I mentioned, Dad ran a tight ship. His main tool for enforcing discipline in 14 kindergarten and grade school classes with approximately 30 students each was a mechanized paddling machine.

Any student making trouble for his teachers would first be informed in a one-on-one session with the principal about the possibilities of an appointment with the paddling machine. It allegedly resided somewhere in the principal's office. Keep in mind this was a period when paddling a misbehaving student was allowed.

Principal Corban Goble and his teaching faculty, Lincoln Elementary School, Pittsburg, Kansas, circa 1962.

Of course, the mechanical paddling machine did not exist. The mere threat of one was more than enough to keep order. I had heard these paddle machine stories from other kids (I attended another grade school due to district policy) and was very curious one day as I quietly opened the mysterious paddle machine closet door for a peek.

Much to my surprise, I found only lots of school supplies stacked neatly. It was a moment of clarity for me. You might call it an epiphany.

Each day during the summer, my Dad would deliver the extra vegetables we grew to his teaching staff and our neighbors. I can still remember how much joy he had in giving fresh corn, tomatoes, green beans and new potatoes to his friends. There was an extra spring in his step as he made his deliveries and I often rode along.

I understand his joy better now. I get that it was much more fun to give away his garden vegetables than it would have been to sell them for a profit.

Making A Difference With Your Career

Early in your career, making a difference can mean building your business, medical or law practice or whatever you are pursuing. The path can take lots of turns, twists and even reach a few dead ends. You have to hang in there.

Buying your first home, starting a family and then seeing your children do well in school are all goals high on most parents' lists of what's important and what making a difference can mean. The uncertainty of what the future might hold, although daunting at times, is part of the fun. As I said earlier, it's the journey that is important, not the destination.

The Sandwich Generation

Taking care of one's parents can also be a difference-maker for many of us and often becomes a high priority once kids are grown and on their way. With improved disease prevention, surgical procedures and better health awareness, Americans are living longer.

I saw recently that the average life span in the U.S. is 76 years for men and 82 years for women. It's easy for the generation in the middle to find itself "sandwiched" between raising children and caring for parents, as we have.

My overall goal in taking care of Mom in her later years was to never have to look back and regret the level of care that I could provide. I saw it as payback time for all the great things she had done for me growing up. Although we lost Dad unexpectedly to heart disease when he was 56, Mom lived to be 96.

By the way, I love the characterization of a mom as a person who when serving the last remaining piece of her famous cherry pie, suddenly declares that she never really cared for cherry pie. That was my Mom.

Simple acts of kindness are one way to pay it forward.

Other Difference-Makers

Helping members of one's extended family achieve things that would not normally be possible for them is also on the make-a-difference list for many. This could mean seeing your children through college and perhaps graduate school, unexpectedly stepping in to help pay college tuition for a grandchild, or perhaps helping with a first down payment on a home.

There are many things, large and small, you can do with a part of your mature nest egg to help other people do extraordinary things.

Ask any coach at a high school near you if someone on his or her team needs help buying the required sports equipment. Trust me, it will feel really good when you are anonymously able to make a little difference for those student athletes so they can better enjoy sports. I look at it like I am making a very small investment in that person's future.

Teachers can always use resources to improve the student experience in their classrooms. If you've had the gift of a good education, like I have, you can pay something forward in this way. You may remember one of Sharon's rules in Chapter 1: Education is the key to one's success.

Helping older neighbors can be very gratifying. Our first home was in Prairie Village, Kansas, a community built by the J.C. Nichols Company of

Country Club Plaza fame for returning WWII veterans, who could use GI Bill loans to buy their first home.

We adopted our next-door neighbors, Charles (Gabby) Gabhart and his wife, Mary. Gabby had served in the Navy (and had the anchor tattoo to prove it), and we thoroughly enjoyed our friendship with this older couple that shared our love of pets.

They were like having a human security system while we were at work. They watched our home like hawks and even let our dogs out over the lunch hour. In their later years, we kept an eye on them and made sure they were getting proper health care and made their doctors' appointments. Helping them helped us.

It is so easy to create acts of kindness. All you have to do is keep your eyes open and opportunities will appear. I really like the Starbucks custom, for example, of anonymously paying for the coffee of the person behind you in line. What a simple and inexpensive way to make a statement about kindness. If you always give, you will always have.

Is There Something More?

One thing I have observed from watching many driven and successful people is that even after building a successful nest egg, raising a family and completing a satisfying career, they often have a strong desire to do something more.

This need often materializes toward the end of a fulfilling career as one contemplates retirement or some variation of it. Work, in many cases, has helped define who we are as individuals, serving as a psychological glue to help us keep our lives in balance.

Not going to work after a long and demanding career may call for a lot of mental preparation and adjustments. Go to a bookstore or online and check out any of the dozen or so new books on the subject.

Yes, I have my own boots-on-the-ground research. I have watched wealthy, successful people experience a letdown, anxiety and even health issues without work or a defined purpose. It is not uncommon for people to mourn what feels like the loss of the personal and professional standing and respect that they've worked so hard to build.

Many of my friends and clients report that after a few fun months of retirement they get really bored!

Although travel, golf, tennis, boating and fishing may sound great while one is working, most people cannot do or afford these things every day in retirement.

My observation is that there has to be something more in order to avoid boredom and a letdown. From watching friends and colleagues, I'm convinced that we should start planning and preparing for this transition before we retire, perhaps as much as a decade before.

Filling The Boredom Gap

The good news is that there are many ways to fill this gap: starting a second career or new business, finding a new interest and running with it, acting as a consultant or director for an organization in your field of interest or expertise, doing volunteer and charitable work, mentoring a younger person in your profession.

This also is the time, in my opinion, to knock out some of the things that remain on your "bucket list." I saw a recent survey of 100-year-olds who were asked the question, what would they have done differently in their lives? The number one answer was, "Don't wait too long to do the things you really want to do." Note to file.

A personal example: I'm writing "Nest Egg" in the final quarter of my career to hopefully fill part of whatever "gap" comes. The Swiss psychiatrist Carl Jung said that all of us have a "life task" that needs to be "actualized" and it occurred to me recently that writing books about investing might be mine.

I would like to give back something before I retire that might make a difference to someone struggling to build his or her financial cushion.

This book so far has seemed the best way to accomplish that. It has taken me seven years to complete. My day job at UMB, thankfully, is still very demanding. My first book, "More Yield, Less Risk...Better Sleep!" also took seven years to finish. I see a pattern here, so perhaps ahead for me is writing more books in the hope that my experience may benefit someone else.

Forrest Gump's Mom Was So Right

I am a Tom Hanks fan and one of my favorite movies is "Forrest Gump." Many of us are familiar with the movie's most famous philosophical quote, when Forrest's Mom says, "Forest, life is like a box of chocolates – you just never know what you are going to get."

In another scene she is counseling Forrest about what is truly important in one's life, when she says, "Forrest, there is only so much fortune a man really needs – and the rest is just for showin' off." I agree with both statements and am thankful for the many great opportunities I have had so far in my life.

Another favorite movie of mine, shown every Christmas, is "It's a Wonderful Life," starring Jimmy Stewart and Donna Reed. On the wall of George Bailey's father's office at the building and loan is a sign that reads: "All you can take with you is that which you have given away."

You just never know what you are going to get, and so far, we have been very fortunate. We followed "Sharon's basic rules" from Chapter 1 and the nest egg risk formula presented in Chapter 3. We took full advantage of 401k matches, IRAs, college funding programs, custodial accounts and gifts to minors, deferred compensation plans and automated investments in stocks.

We have always reinvested dividends and bond coupons rather than spend them, and worked hard to keep our debt low and our lifestyle modest over the past 40 years. We subscribe to the "All cattle, no hat," way of living and managing our finances.

So now, much is expected. I have researched and then selected several charitable organizations in the Kansas City area that I believe are exemplary in their missions, and will donate the royalties, after expenses, from this book to them. (Of course, these are a small fraction of the effective, life-saving organizations here.) My hope is that something extraordinary will happen because of this.

My Personal List

Ozanam
This organization has served the Kansas City area for over 65 years and provides residential and educational day treatment programs for boys and girls, ages 12-18. The majority of children treated at Ozanam have suffered abuse, abandonment, neglect and other types of trauma.

ozanam.org

Operation Breakthrough
Its mission is to help children living in poverty in the urban core develop to their fullest potential. Operation Breakthrough empowers and supports families through advocacy, referral services and emergency aid. It serves more than 400 children daily.

operationbreakthrough.org

Chain of Hope KC
This organization helps lower income individuals by covering veterinary care and other expenses for their pets. If there is mistreatment, Chain of Hope provides medical assistance and often attempts to place the animal in a more responsible home. It protects animals because they "have no voice."

chainofhopekc.org

Rose Brooks Domestic Violence Center
Rose Brooks provides emergency services for women and children who have experienced fear and violence in their own homes. Their mission is to break the cycle of domestic violence by providing emergency shelter, counseling, health care, and help to rebuild their lives. They maintain a staffed phone line.

rosebrooks.org

Wayside Waifs

The mission of this animal welfare organization and shelter is to place adoptable animals in responsible homes. Founded in 1940 as a Society for The Prevention of Cruelty to Animals, it became Wayside Waifs in 1944. It remains one of the largest no kill pet adoption centers in Kansas City.

waysidewaifs.org

Habitat for Humanity

Habitat for Humanity has been making home ownership a reality for families since 1979. Over 300 homes have been built by volunteers in targeted Kansas City neighborhoods.

habitatkc.org

City Union Mission

At 1100 E. 11th Street, City Union Mission has provided food and warm beds for thousands of poverty-stricken men, women and children since 1924. Relief includes distribution of food, clothing, school supplies, household items and utility assistance.

cityunionmission.org

PEARLS OF WISDOM

You never see Brinks armored trucks in funeral processions. You can't take it with you.

The Search For The Extraordinary

I hope you have enjoyed reading "Nest Egg" and that at least some of the suggestions will help you in your lifetime nest egg building process.

If you start as early as you can, invest regularly, are patient and calm when markets drop, avoid excessive concentrations, and recheck your risk formula at least annually, history shows you should be good to go financially when retirement arrives. Remember, compound interest is your friend!

I also hope you find as I have that it's even more gratifying to donate a portion of your nest egg on a regular basis to extraordinary causes than it was to build it in the first place.

Create Some Gamma Ray Bursts

With regards to your brain, I strongly encourage you to break from your work at least a few minutes each day to create some gamma ray bursts, also known as epiphanies. Let your mind wander and daydream a little. The benefits can be significant. In that state, neuroscientists say, you are actually creating more neural connections in your brain, leading to more moments of insightful clarity that will help you keep things in perspective and enjoy your life's journey even more.

I would like to leave you with four simple wishes: May you always have warmth for your home, oil for your lantern, laughter every day of your life and peace in your heart.

ACKNOWLEDGMENTS

I would like to thank the following individuals, without whom "Nest Egg" would not have been possible:

Doug Weaver, my publisher with Kansas City Star Books, for his interest in this project and wise counsel. He always places my best interest first, and that philosophy makes him very successful as a publisher. He is a gentleman.

Carol Powers, who as my editor evinced the patience of Job. Carol's extensive background in journalism was incredibly helpful to me. She is a real pro.

Brian Grubb, whose feel for tone and stylish design concepts were evident from the beginning. I am profoundly grateful for his graphic expertise and professionalism.

R. Crosby Kemper, Jr., who we sadly lost in 2014. He gave me my start as a trainee at United Missouri Bank in 1981. He was a mentor for me throughout my career and I learned a great deal from him about judging character and doing the right thing. He was a very generous man who was in favor of anything that made Kansas City a better place to work, live and raise a family.

Mariner Kemper, who leads UMB now and is Crosby's third son. He is much like his father in being a principled and great leader. Just as significant is his sense of fairness and compassion, as well as the importance he places on being a good husband and dad. Mariner, himself an artist, supports creativity and the role of specialists at UMB, which is a lucky thing for me.

Peter de Silva, UMB Financial Corporation's chief operating officer, for his enthusiastic support of both of my books. Peter is one of the most honest, fair and dedicated men I have ever met. He still finds time, somehow, to be a great husband and dad, which I admire greatly. We are so lucky at UMB that Crosby convinced Peter to move to Kansas City from Boston and join us in 2005. What a difference he has made for our company.

Harold "Hal" Hollister, executive vice president of the UMB investment banking division, who taught me how to know more about a client's investments than the client could possibly ever know. His pre-computer, handwritten analyses of clients' portfolios were the foundation of the analysis we still perform today. Hal also recommended me for an instructorship at the graduate school of banking at the University of Wisconsin in Madison in 1986. I am still on the faculty today, as I enjoy teaching very much, and it is a way for me to give back to the banking industry and honor other teachers in our family, including my Dad.

Byron G. Thompson, who passed away recently, was my first boss at UMB after I completed the management training program. He was my first mentor and taught me about dedication and how to behave in a professional manner and treat people with respect. He had a thousand motivational quips that are still quoted regularly by many of those he mentored. He was a great man and made a difference in the lives of many.

Lyle Wells, another great banker and mentor of mine at UMB, who was vice chairman when he passed away in December 2013. I learned first hand from Lyle and his wife, Ann, the importance of strong professional and personal relationships, as Lyle and I travelled the UMB "territory" together for decades. Ann defined the term "hostess with the mostest." It was a privilege to watch Lyle and Ann in action with our clients. People were drawn to them because of their humility, warmth and sincerity.

Esther Smith, my piano teacher, who drilled in me, when I started lessons as a kindergartner, the importance of repetition, memorization and attention to every minute detail in order for a piano solo to be perfect. I cannot say I always enjoyed my daily practice sessions but she took my love of music to a new level. I now play the piano every day for relaxation, especially when the markets are volatile. My wife, Sharon, says she can tell how the markets performed by how loudly I play.

Larry Garman, my high school football coach, who taught me that it is possible to give 105 percent to something very important to you. The extra 5 percent, he said, was something I had to find within myself...and may not realize even exists. In other words, there are some things in life so important that they require more focus and effort than you knew was possible. These are, most assuredly, the things to pursue.

Ernest Nelson, my 10th grade biology teacher, who awakened me scholastically and taught me how to compete in academics. Each day, using a magic marker, he ceremoniously posted everyone's grades on a chart in the front of his classroom. This teaching style isn't allowed in high schools today due to privacy issues, unfortunately. You never, ever dared come to his class unprepared or sleepy. Mr. Nelson is probably the reason for my interest in science and why my undergraduate college degree turned out to be human biology.

Wesley Cunningham, my seventh grade math teacher and basketball coach, for making math so fun and interesting. He made it a competitive challenge to solve math problems, which also taught us about the discipline of trusting a formula. Little did I know that his enthusiasm would lead to many more college math courses, which later would make bonds and financial instruments much easier for me to understand. He took the fear of math away.

J. Chris Perryman, M.D., our family physician at St. Luke's Hospital, for caring for my family for over 30 years. Dr. Perryman is one of the busiest yet most caring physicians in Kansas City, who still finds time at the start of his day for prayer and meditation. A graduate of Yale University and the University of Kansas Medical School, he inspires me to be a better person... and uses his great sense of humor to help me through my dreaded annual checkups.

Reverends Robert Meneilly and Tom Are, my spiritual gurus. We have been members of the Village Presbyterian Church in Prairie Village, Kansas, for over 30 years. These two incredibly gifted speakers and spiritual leaders have pushed me to see many things from a more compassionate point of view. They also help me to keep the focus on the things that are truly important and lasting. Tom always says that if you can count it, it does not count. He is so right.

I would also like to thank my partners in the investment banking division at UMB: Mary Michael, Stephen Dumont and Maria Bryant. Mary and I have worked together for 30 years and she epitomizes the UMB brand with her integrity, honesty, and by always placing clients' best interests first. Maria and Stephen share this passion.

My 15 seconds of fame

A perk of participating in Opening Bell ceremonies at the NASDAQ MarketSite in Times Square is seeing your-self seven stories high on the cylindrical video tower that wraps the NASDAQ building.

REFERENCES

The images in this book, except those sourced by page number below, are from stock houses, the author's personal collection, or are the work of the designer.

12	AP
15	The Kansas City Star
17	Dairy Queen
19	Oaktree Capital Management
26	Vanguard
31	Bloomberg
36	Jeremy Siegel
38	"Stocks for the Long Run"
39	Dow Jones Monday Morning
40	"Stocks for the Long Run"
41	Federal Reserve Bank
43	Bank News Media (chart)
	Federal Reserve (Yellen)
57	Bloomberg
71	Bank News Media
82	Union Plus Retirement Planning Center
102	University of Virginia
110, 111	UMB Bank archives
115, 116, 117	Boca Raton Regional Hospital
118	Christine Lynn
122	UMB Bank
123	Kansas City Symphony, photo by Brian Rice
126	UMB Bank Collection
127, 129	© Thomas Jefferson Foundation at Monticello, photo by Harlow Chandler
146	NASDAQ

NOTES